What people are saying about
A DEVOTIONAL WALK WITH FORGIVENESS

A Devotional Walk with Forgiveness is a thorough, practical treatment of forgiveness. I appreciated Judy's approach in seeing forgiveness as a daily spiritual exercise that keeps us fit in our relationship with God and with those persons God has placed around us. Often times it is easy to treat a subject like this on a theoretical level, but not provide the practical recommendations needed to make forgiveness real in our lives. Thanks, Judy, for your desire to help the church practice this very important teaching of Christ Jesus. — **Rev. Daniel R. Siems, Senior Pastor, First Baptist Church of Galesburg, Illinois**

* * *

Forgiveness is at the heart of the Christian faith. On the cross Jesus prayed, "Father, forgive them for they do not know what they are doing." We are taught to confess our sins in order to obtain divine forgiveness. Yet, most of us are not good at forgiving others for the hurts they have inflicted upon us. Our lack of forgiveness poisons our souls and hinders relationships. While books on the topic abound, little attention is given to the "how to" of forgiveness. This "how to" is Judith Ingram's valuable contribution in *A Devotional Walk with Forgiveness*. Adopting the health fitness "workout" metaphor, we are guided on a five-week interactive daily exercise program of spiritual fitness focused upon incorporating forgiveness into our spiritual lives as a consistent, ongoing practice. — **Dr. M. James Sawyer, Th.M., Director of Sacred Saga Ministries, professor, author of *The Survivor's Guide to Theology*, co-author of *Reinventing Jesus* with J. Ed Komoszewski and Daniel B. Wallace, and co-editor of *Who's Afraid of the Holy Spirit?***

Judith Ingram

A Devotional Walk with Forgiveness
Daily Exercise for Spiritual Fitness

Judith Ingram

Vinspire Spirit
A Division of Vinspire Publishing
Ladson, South Carolina
www.vinspirepublishing.com

ISBN: 978-0-9834198-2-2

PUBLISHED BY VINSPIRE SPIRIT, A DIVISION OF VINSPIRE
PUBLISHING, LLC

I dedicate this book to
Ruth Ann Thompson
who always believed in its worth
and to
Frank Ingram
who always believed in mine

Contents

INTRODUCTION

Get Ready to Walk!

Spend your time and energy in the exercise of keeping spiritually fit. Bodily exercise is all right, but spiritual exercise is much more important and is a tonic for all you do. So exercise yourself spiritually and practice being a better Christian, because that will help you not only now in this life but in the next life too. This is the truth and everyone should accept it. (1 Timothy 4:7-9, TLB)

Is God challenging you to become more spiritually fit?

This book is your invitation to train for five weeks with an expert on spiritual fitness: *forgiveness*. To be spiritually fit means to be actively engaged in learning more about God and practicing how to be like Him and how to be more fully human in Him. Spiritual fitness grows with regular spiritual exercise. Prayer, meditation, Bible study, worship, confession, service, and obedience to God's teachings — all these practices help us to know God, to love Him more deeply, and to honor each other and ourselves as reflections of His perfect image.

Is equipping yourself to follow God wherever He leads a goal that appeals to you?

If you agree to the training, forgiveness will accompany you on your daily walk, helping you to observe yourself and offering relationship advice from a biblical perspective. To get the most from your training, give yourself at least fifteen minutes each day to read a new chapter and consider the challenge questions. Let forgiveness speak to you during your daily activities, your prayer time, and your conversations with other people. Open your mind and unlock your heart, with its memories of hurt and betrayal, to the possibility that you can forgive what today may seem unforgivable.

Be advised that this training is not without risk. Forgiveness is more than a feeling; it is a spiritual lifestyle. God will use this study to align your heart with His and your life with His purpose *if* you are willing to be challenged and to be changed.

Some of the reading you will accept as intuitive, but some of it will raise questions and even defensiveness. Expect resistance! Forgiveness will offer advice that contradicts much of what you have learned about how to handle relationship dilemmas. For the next five weeks, give yourself the freedom to consider different solutions. Take time to imagine what your life would be like if you became a more forgiving person.

How to Use This Book

Your five-week walk is divided into brief daily chapters designed to introduce forgiveness principles and offer opportunities for you to practice them. At the end of each chapter you will find an activity section called **Today's Fitness Challenge**, which will help you summarize and think about the principles presented:

☑ FEED YOUR SOUL revitalizes your walk with wise words from Scripture and selected quotations.

☑ LISTEN TO FORGIVENESS reinforces the lesson with a summary statement that you can repeat during the day.

☑ CHECK YOUR HEART presents a question to help you evaluate the condition of your heart and your readiness to forgive.

☑ KEEP GOING encourages you to practice the lesson principle with a commitment statement.

The **Bonus Challenge** questions can further help you to explore the day's lesson. Each week of five chapters concludes with a review sheet, **My Fitness Log,** and an intensive exercise called **Weekend Workout** to help you dig deeper and stretch your spiritual muscles.

Equip Yourself for the Walk

The lessons are designed for personal study but easily adapt to partner or small group study as well. Appendix C offers suggestions for training with forgiveness in a small group setting. However you choose to pursue your study, make sure you have a notebook for jotting down your answers, thoughts, and questions, and a Bible for looking up verses. A concordance is helpful for following up on topics that God is urging you to think more about.

Be aware that learning to forgive is a process. It is a transformation of heart that requires time, patience, and diligence. Give yourself the full five weeks or longer if you need it to complete the study. Take time every day to sit quietly with the Spirit and open yourself to the nurture and healing of God's personal word for you.

Tell others what you are trying to accomplish by walking with forgiveness. Ask loved ones for their support as you try out new ways of responding to injury. Be prepared for criticism from those who hold firmly to their unforgiving attitudes. They are invested in your failure — don't let them discourage you!

A serious walk with forgiveness inevitably stirs up uncomfortable feelings. If you are not studying with a group, then choose a friend, a prayer partner, or a counselor to consult with regularly as you journey through these five weeks. Choose someone who will speak truth to you and will listen to your reflections without judging. Ask him or her to help you keep a healthy perspective as you navigate painful memories and old feelings. If at any time you feel overwhelmed by the readings or the feelings they bring up, *stop reading* and consult with a pastor or a counselor. You may have uncovered issues of trauma or loss that require special care before you can continue your walk with forgiveness.

Most importantly, invite forgiveness into your prayer life. Ask God to show you what it means to forgive and what it means for *you* to forgive. He knows your heart and He knows your wounds. Allow Him to care for you and to supply you with the strength and wisdom you need as you seek change. He is waiting to work a miracle in your life!

Forget the former things; do not dwell on the past. See, I am doing a new thing! Now it springs up; do you not perceive it? I am making a way in the desert and streams in the wasteland. (Isaiah 43:18-19)

PART ONE

Understanding Forgiveness

Whether you turn to the right or to the left, your ears will hear a voice behind you, saying, "This is the way; walk in it."

Isaiah 30:21

Week One

The path of the righteous is like the first gleam of dawn,
shining ever brighter till the full light of day.
But the way of the wicked is like deep darkness;
they do not know what makes them stumble. (Proverbs 4:18-19)

Week One
Day 1

What Is Forgiveness?

But I say to you that listen, Love your enemies, do good to those who hate you, bless those who curse you, pray for those who abuse you. If anyone strikes you on the cheek, offer the other also; and from anyone who takes away your coat do not withhold even your shirt. Give to everyone who begs from you; and if anyone takes away your goods, do not ask for them again. Do to others as you would have them do to you.

If you love those who love you, what credit is that to you? For even sinners love those who love them. If you do good to those who do good to you, what credit is that to you? For even sinners do the same. (Luke 6:27-33, NRSV)

To forgive is to act on the decision to bless and not curse your offender.

In becoming a student of forgiveness, you have taken on a significant task. One can make the case that the entire Bible is about forgiveness—God's plan from the beginning to love and redeem all of His creation. Through the sacrifice of His Son on the cross, God forgives our sins and calls us back into relationship with Him. Furthermore, He makes it clear that we are to follow His example and forgive one another: "Bear with each other and forgive whatever grievances you may have against one another. Forgive as the Lord forgave you."[1]

It's a tall order. And if we are to obey this command, we must first understand what forgiveness means.

Our definition of forgiveness identifies its five parts: *acting* on the *decision* to *bless* and *not curse* your *offender*. Each part is described below and discussed further in the next few chapters.

Forgiveness is a call to action. Forgiveness without observable action is incomplete. We must find ways to demonstrate to our offender as well as to others that we have cast off malice and adopted an attitude of goodwill toward the person who hurt us. We make forgiveness *visible*.

Forgiveness is a decision. Feelings are important, but we can't rely on them to get us through the forgiveness process. Wounded feelings are often unpredictable and difficult to control. To obey God and forgive the person who hurt us, despite how we may sometimes feel about it, requires a conscious decision to change. We *choose* to forgive.

Forgiveness is blessing the wrongdoer. In forgiving, we endorse whatever is in our offender's best interests. To bless is not merely to let go of negativity but to deliberately cultivate benevolence toward the other person. We adopt *goodwill intentions*.

Forgiveness is giving up malice. Most people rightly associate forgiveness with letting go of bitterness, resentment, and hatred. We instinctively know that cursing others is neither healthy nor productive, and in forgiving, we take back our curses. We let go of *malicious intentions*.

Forgiveness is acknowledging that harm was done because someone acted unjustly. A first step in forgiving is to identify the offense and the offender. It's important to understand that God does not ask us to forgive the terrible things that people do to us, but He does ask us to forgive the people who do them. Adultery, rape, and murder are not redeemable, but in God's kingdom adulterers, rapists, and murderers are. We forgive a *person*.

Although we want to obey God's call to forgive others, our efforts can be hampered by confusion and misconceptions about forgiveness. Often people are reluctant to forgive because their assumptions about forgiveness make it unpalatable. Forgiving may seem like ignoring, excusing, or even condoning a wrongful action that should be exposed and punished.

A common misconception is that only weak or passive people forgive. Some victims fear that forgiving will make them vulnerable to further hurt or allow others to be hurt. Forgiving may seem like admitting defeat and letting the perpetrator win.

Identifying misconceptions about forgiveness helps us to clarify what it truly means:

Forgiveness does not deny what happened. When we forgive, we acknowledge a wrongful act, identify the wrongdoer, and choose to extend mercy anyway.

Forgiveness does not justify or excuse the offense. Although we may understand the circumstances and why the offender acted wrongfully, we acknowledge that the act was nevertheless wrong.

Forgiveness does not pardon the offender. Judges and those in authority can grant mercy and release the guilty from punishment; in contrast, forgiveness extends mercy from one sinner to another, acknowledging our equality before God.

Forgiveness does not condone what happened. We disapprove of the offending behavior; yet we choose to release the offender from our censure.

Forgiveness does not sanction unrepentant behavior. Although we release the offender from personal penalty for past offenses, we are sensible about protecting ourselves and others from further hurtful acts; we support legal and moral authorities' efforts to uphold justice.

Forgiveness does not trust blindly. Even if we forgive, it may take time to rebuild trust; if the offender does not demonstrate efforts to change, trust may never be reestablished.

Forgiveness does not necessarily lead to reconciliation.

Although our forgiveness may open the door to rebuilding a damaged relationship, reconciliation requires the efforts of both the offender and the forgiver.

The passage from Luke that introduces this chapter begins with these words: "But I say to you that listen..." *The Message* translates it, "To you who are ready for the truth, I say this..." Not everyone wants to hear what Jesus had to say about loving our enemies. His ideas run counter to our worldly wisdom and natural inclinations. However, if you picked up this book because you want to learn more about forgiving, and if you've made it this far into the text, then Jesus is speaking to *you*. Take heart! Not only have you decided to take that spiritual walk with forgiveness, but you are already traveling the path. And God will reward you by working a holy miracle in you—He will reshape your heart until it is a perfect reflection of His loving and forgiving nature: "Your reward will be great, and you will be children of the Most High; for he is kind to the ungrateful and the wicked. Be merciful, just as your Father is merciful."[2]

Today's Fitness Challenge - Day 1

☑ FEED YOUR SOUL: *"Nothing in this world bears the impress of the Son of God so surely as forgiveness."*
— Alice Cary, American poet

☑ LISTEN TO FORGIVENESS: To the extent that I feel loved and forgiven by God, I can love and forgive others.

☑ CHECK YOUR HEART: What reasons have I given myself that justify my refusing to forgive?

☑ KEEP GOING: With God's help, I will open myself to learning more about what forgiveness means.

Bonus Challenge

1. In naming a personal injury that I have not been able to forgive, which of the five parts of forgiveness was I unable to apply? Which part would be the easiest first step toward forgiving this person?

2. Why does God want me to love my enemies and to do good to those who wish me harm? Who would benefit if I could obey these commands?

3. What do I hope to learn during this five-week walk with forgiveness? Be specific.

Week One
Day 2

Bless Your Persecutors

Bless those who persecute you; bless and do not curse. Rejoice with those who rejoice; mourn with those who mourn. Live in harmony with one another....Do not repay anyone evil for evil. Be careful to do what is right in the eyes of everybody. If it is possible, as far as it depends on you, live at peace with everyone. Do not take revenge, my friends, but leave room for God's wrath, for it is written: "It is mine to avenge; I will repay," says the Lord. (Romans 12:14-19)

Learning to forgive means learning to bless and not curse those who offend you.

When God asks you to forgive, He will always give you the grace and the goodness to do it. Don't ever think that you are alone in your efforts. God has promised you a way out of your anger and bitterness if you are willing to submit to the wise counsel of His Spirit, who lives every moment with you and never lies to you about what you should say or do.[1]

Others around you may not understand what you are trying to accomplish. They may criticize you or even try to block your efforts to forgive. Blessing the person who hurt you makes no sense to those who have never experienced God's forgiveness. At times when you are tempted to give up the effort, it helps to remember *why* you are forgiving. The simple reason is that God commands it; the deeper reason is in wanting to follow the merciful God who pursued you with such love—He met you while you were still in sin and rebellion, an enemy of Himself.[2]

He surrounded you with His love, washed you clean with the sacrifice of His Son, and showered you with grace.[3] He made your body a holy temple for His Spirit and adopted you into His family.[4] Moreover, He appointed you to a holy priesthood and gave you the *responsibility* to bless others with the same goodness and love He freely gives you.[5]

God's grace carries momentum, a kind of divine energy that keeps it moving from one being to another. The love He gives you He intends for you to share with others; His forgiveness of you becomes your motivation to forgive. To be a part of His kingdom means to participate in His tireless pursuit of the lost by loving and forgiving them, even while they are still scornful and rebellious, and offering them the hope of heaven.

The Gospel of Matthew introduces Jesus' Sermon on the Mount with a passage we know as the Beatitudes.[6] The passage gives eight depictions of how we are blessed (*beati*) when we embrace the righteous life. The word "blessed" can be translated "happy" or "fortunate," but being blessed by God is not the same as *feeling* happy or fortunate; it is being happy or fortunate *in God's sight* and *by His measure*. His rewards to us may not be what our worldly culture values or even recognizes.

The Beatitudes are examples of how God measures and rewards righteous living. Each beatitude is described below, along with a suggestion for how we can pass along the blessing.

"Blessed are the poor in spirit, for theirs is the kingdom of heaven." The "poor in spirit" are those who are aware of their sin and acknowledge that they have no righteousness of their own to make them worthy of God's grace. Their spirits are empty, and they trust Jesus to make them whole and acceptable to God. The Father rewards their humility with full citizenship in His kingdom. ***Blessing others:*** When we are truthful about our own sin and unworthiness, we are free to see others in their sin and unworthiness and love them just as they are.

"Blessed are those who mourn, for they will be comforted." As children of the kingdom, we mourn our fallen nature and our failure to keep God's laws. We also mourn for the sorrow we bring to God by our sin and the dishonor we bring to His name. The blessing for us is that godly sorrow for our sin brings us to repentance, and we will be comforted in the presence of the Lamb when "God will wipe away every tear from their eyes."[7] ***Blessing others***: When we see others who are in trouble, we can comfort them with the same comfort that we ourselves receive from God.

"Blessed are the meek, for they will inherit the earth." The meek in God are as Jesus described Himself, "gentle and humble in heart."[9] The meek empty themselves of their own importance and fill themselves with the heart and will of God. With patient, long-sighted faithfulness, they claim nothing for themselves but work to advance God's agenda. As a reward, they are promised a share in the kingdom when Christ reigns over the entire earth. ***Blessing others***: Patience, kindness, gentleness, humility — when we bring these traits into our relationships, we can soothe tempers, promote trust, improve communications, and demonstrate our caring.

"Blessed are those who hunger and thirst for righteousness, for they will be filled." We are blessed when we passionately pursue whatever is just and honorable and Christ-like. The righteousness we hope to attain may be holiness in our personal lives, fair and ethical dealings in our community and government, or God's redemption of the whole world. Such righteousness is beyond our power to produce but is given to us by God as a reward for our faithful pursuit. ***Blessing others***: When we long for righteous living above every selfish intention, our treatment of others becomes increasingly honorable, ethical, fair, and generous.

"Blessed are the merciful, for they will be shown mercy."

Mercy is a loving attention to the neediness, misery, sorrow, pain, or despair we see in others. We are merciful when we recognize others' distress, feel compassion for them, and somehow work to ease their suffering. To be capable of extending mercy, we must first recognize our own neediness and open our hearts to God's healing mercies, which He gives us daily, and to the saving mercy He has promised to us on the day of Christ's return.[10] *Blessing others*: When God eases our suffering, He opens our eyes to the suffering of others and gives us the love and the means to help them.

"Blessed are the pure in heart, for they will see God." Spiritual purity begins on the inside. It is the absence of sin and an undivided devotion to God. The pure in heart pray with the psalmist: "Create in me a pure heart, O God, and renew a steadfast spirit within me."[11] Purity of heart is clear evidence of God's presence in our lives because only He can wash away our sin. The Bible promises that the pure in heart will see God, both in eternity and now, through our faith in the person of Jesus. *Blessing others*: When our hearts are pure, we reflect God's loving nature in every aspect of our lives, including our thoughts, attitudes, and behaviors toward others.

"Blessed are the peacemakers, for they will be called children of God." Peacemakers are genuine imitators of Christ. They take to heart His mission to mend the rifts that separate people from God and from each other. Through His death on the cross, Christ reconciled us to God, and we who call Him Lord become God's true children.[12] *Blessing others*: When Christ becomes our peace through His blood, we accept His calling to become instruments of peace and reconciliation in our relationships.

"Blessed are those who are persecuted because of righteousness, for theirs is the kingdom of heaven." The persecuted mentioned here suffer because they are devoted to

God's kingdom and to spreading the good news of Christ risen. The world under Satan's control bitterly opposes anyone who furthers God's efforts to redeem the lost and establish peace. God rewards those who suffer for living a righteous life by securing for them a place in His kingdom. ***Blessing others***: When we are persecuted for trying to live a life worthy of God's kingdom, our steadfastness in the face of suffering gives witness to our persecutors that we serve a God who is bigger than the evil in this world and the misery that they suffer from their own sin.

Forgiveness offers us many opportunities to bless our offender with the blessings God has given to us. It's important to remember that we have no righteousness of our own or even the *will* to forgive. All our goodness, including our good intentions, come from God's own heart. Our joy is to make ourselves available to His Spirit and go wherever He has healing work for us to do.

Today's Fitness Challenge - Day 2

☑ FEED YOUR SOUL: *"You are royal priests, a holy nation, God's very own possession. As a result, you can show others the goodness of God, for he called you out of the darkness into his wonderful light."*

— 1 Peter 2:9 (NLT)

☑ LISTEN TO FORGIVENESS: God blesses me twice when I share His goodness with others.

☑ CHECK YOUR HEART: When I think about blessing my offender, what feelings come up for me?

☑ KEEP GOING: With God's help, I will look for opportunities to act in the best interests of the person who offended me.

Bonus Challenge

1. Do I feel blessed by God? How is being blessed "in God's sight and by His measure" different from what I consider to be "happy" or "fortunate"?

2. What would others think of me if I suddenly developed a goodwill attitude toward my offender? Who would support my efforts? Who would be least likely to understand my change in attitude?

3. Have I ever received kindness from someone when I was expecting anger or criticism? How did the unexpected blessing make me feel? How did I respond?

Week One
Day 3

Bitter Roots

Make every effort to live in peace with all men and to be holy; without holiness no one will see the Lord. See to it that no one misses the grace of God and that no bitter root grows up to cause trouble and defile many. (Hebrews 12:14-15)

It is impossible for you to bless others while your heart is still cursing them.

In the apostle Paul's letter to the Roman church, he tells Christians to bless those who persecute them; he then adds, "bless and do not curse."[1] According to Paul, the two halves of responding to personal injury are (a) to act in godly ways and (b) to *refrain* from acting in *ungodly* ways. Paul was very familiar with the struggle we all face in wanting to act in ways that please God but also craving satisfaction for the injustices we suffer.[2] We can little afford to meet our offender's needs when we are consumed with outrage over the offense and plotting how we can get even. If we are to be holy, Paul says, we must give up *un*-holiness and allow no bitter root to grow up and cause trouble in our relationship.

Bitter roots are malicious attitudes and behaviors that develop after the effects of the injury have had some time to settle in. We create them out of our *primary* emotions, such as anger, hurt, grief, disappointment, and fear. These primary emotions are part of our emergency response kit that we pull out automatically when we are confronted with unexpected crisis or injury. God gives us these emotions to help us cope — they alert us to the possibility of danger or violation of a personal boundary; they call up experiences from our past that can help us to quickly assess the situation and recall how different strategies worked; and they mobilize us to take responsive action.

As useful and necessary as they are, however, primary emotions are intended to be short-lived. If they stay around too long, if we feed them and protect them and keep them alive, then they turn destructive. They crowd out goodness by taking hold of our hearts and putting down roots:

Anger becomes **hatred**, an intense loathing that blocks our ability to feel compassion or empathy for our offender.

Hurt becomes **victimhood**, a state in which our sense of self is limited and defined primarily by the injury we suffered.

Grief becomes **despair**, a deep sense of abandonment, hopelessness, or betrayal that generalizes beyond our offender to include other aspects of our life, including God.

Disappointment becomes **resentment** or **bitterness**, a self-righteous indignation at our offender's failure to meet our expectations or moral or ethical standards.

Fear becomes **demonization**, a dehumanizing exaggeration of our offender's negative qualities and power to harm us or others.

These destructive emotions are corruptions of the good and useful primary emotions that God gives us. They are called *secondary* because we create them ourselves when we allow our sin nature to dominate our response to an offense. They serve no good purpose but keep us locked in our hostilities and pain. They are the curse, the ungodly ways of which Paul warns us.

Cursing is the moral and practical opposite of blessing. Our desire to curse others often stems from the misery we experience when we live in defiance of God's laws and without His grace in our lives. The previous chapter describes the eight Beatitudes and how each blessing in turn can bless our relationships. In like manner, the misery we bring on ourselves through sin can bring misery to others as well. The following table describes these same Beatitudes "in reverse."

Blessed are...	Miserable are...
the poor in spirit	the proud, the boastful, the self-reliant — *they are easily offended and quick to criticize others.*
those who mourn	those who seek pleasure and are not bothered by their sin — *they expect satisfaction in this world and resent others who do not provide it.*
the meek	the self-important — *they sacrifice relationships in exchange for power and admiration.*
those who hunger and thirst for righteousness	those who crave what the world values — wealth, sex, status, etc. — *they cheat and betray others to satisfy their cravings.*
the merciful	those who will not admit their need for mercy — *they are blind to others' suffering and selfish with their possessions.*
the pure in heart	those who have no use for God — *they live by their own self-serving rules.*

the peacemakers	the competitive, the aggressive, those who stir up trouble — *they find ways to divide loyalties and escalate conflict.*
those who are persecuted because of righteousness	those who go along with sin because they won't risk antagonizing others — *they cannot be relied on to act uprightly, honestly, or to maintain loyalty in the face of adversity.*

Learning to forgive means learning to rely more and more on God's ways and less on our natural inclinations as we navigate conflict and deal with interpersonal wounds.

Today's Fitness Challenge - Day 3

☑ FEED YOUR SOUL: *"Go ahead and be angry. You do well to be angry – but don't use your anger as fuel for revenge. And don't stay angry. Don't go to bed angry. Don't give the Devil that kind of foothold in your life."*

—Ephesians 4:26-27 (MSG)

☑ LISTEN TO FORGIVENESS: I make my own suffering worse when I allow bitter roots to take hold of my heart.

☑ CHECK YOUR HEART: Which of the five primary emotions mentioned am I most likely to feed and indulge? What happens when it puts down roots in my life?

☑ KEEP GOING: With God's help, I will weed out the bitter roots that keep me from forgiving.

Bonus Challenge

1. What do I think of the statement: "Our desire to curse others often stems from the misery we experience when we live in defiance of God's laws and without His grace in our lives"? How is my opinion shaped by my experience?

2. How does a useful primary emotion like fear become destructive? What does the Bible teach about how to handle each of the five emotions: anger, hurt, grief, disappointment, and fear?

3. When did I allow a bitter root in me to cause trouble in a relationship? Who was hurt by my choices? What would I do differently next time?

Week One
Day 4

Do Good

For God called you to do good, even if it means suffering, just as Christ suffered for you. He is your example, and you must follow in his steps.
    He never sinned,
        nor ever deceived anyone.
    He did not retaliate when he was insulted,
        nor threaten revenge when he suffered.
    He left his case in the hands of God,
        who always judges fairly.
    He personally carried our sins
        in his body on the cross
    so that we can be dead to sin
        and live for what is right.
    By his wounds
        you are healed.
    Once you were like sheep
        who wandered away.
    But now you have turned to your Shepherd,
        the Guardian of your souls. (1 Peter 2:21-25, NLT)

Decide to forgive your offender and then act like it.

The two go hand-in-hand: *acting* on the *decision* to forgive. Of what use is deciding to "bless and not curse"[1] your offender if you continue to hurt and malign him every chance you get? Changes of the mind and heart are only visible to others through our behaviors. Indeed, James, the brother of Jesus, spoke boldly about the importance of acting out our beliefs: *Isn't it obvious that God-talk without God-acts is outrageous nonsense?...You can no more show me your works apart from your faith than I can show you my faith apart from my works. Faith and works, works and faith, fit together hand in glove.*[2]

If you tell your offender "I forgive you" but continue to act the part of a wounded martyr, your "forgiven" offender won't believe you. Conversely, if you change your habits—say good things instead of bad about your offender, rejoice when your offender is blessed rather than when he is suffering, pray for his salvation instead of his damnation, help him to succeed rather than to fail—your offender, as well as others who observe you, will rightly conclude that your heart has been changed. Your actions make your attitudes visible and verifiable.

Because we live in a fallen world, we frequently must choose how we will respond to the selfish acts of people around us, to injustice, persecution, and slander, or to being used or abused by people we love and trust. We may decide to forgive because we are tired of being tense or angry or depressed all the time. We may wish to ease physical ailments, such as headaches, high blood pressure, stomach pain, or troubled sleep, that are aggravated by unresolved conflicts. We may want to break free from painful or frightening memories that keep us trapped in the past. We may want to reclaim the energy that gets lost in ruminating about our injury and replaying in our heads what we could or should have done differently.

All these reasons for deciding to forgive are legitimate. Followers of Christ, however, have an additional reason that can be even more compelling: we forgive those who offend us because God forgave us, and we want, more than anything, to live a life that pleases God. Our deciding to forgive becomes nothing less than inevitable; we know we must forgive because our Lord calls us to do it.

Having decided to forgive, we now must ask what forgiving looks like. The Scripture passage that introduces this chapter gives us the answer: God instructs us to do good by following in the footsteps of Jesus. We make our forgiveness visible when we make our actions conform to the example Jesus gave us as He lived incarnate with us. The passage outlines His footsteps for us:

"He never sinned, nor ever deceived anyone." Jesus always obeyed God, and He always told the truth. In forgiving, we act on the truth that God gives us through His Word and through His Spirit. We are not afraid to see things as they really are or to speak the truth out loud.

"He did not retaliate when he was insulted, nor threaten revenge when he suffered." Jesus did not take insults personally but was able to see into the hearts of those who insulted Him. He suffered cruelly but would not return evil for evil. In forgiving, we deflect insults by remembering that we are chosen and loved by God, the sovereign Lord of the universe. We don't get even or push back because we can't serve God by adding more darkness and misery to the world.

"He left his case in the hands of God, who always judges fairly." Jesus demonstrated His complete trust in the Father to be the righteous Judge who vindicates the moral order of the world and condemns the wicked. In forgiving, we do not judge others because we know that we are just as guilty and unrighteous before God as the worst of our adversaries; it is only through Christ's blood that we have been declared righteous and holy.

"He personally carried our sins in his body on the cross so that we can be dead to sin and live for what is right." Jesus' death on the cross was an atoning sacrifice, that is, a *covering* for our sins so that when the Father looks at us, He sees Christ's righteousness. In forgiving, we cover our offender with our love so that, when we look, we no longer see the offense but only the person.

"By his wounds you are healed." Jesus died for everyone's sins as part of God's plan to redeem the world. In forgiving, we remember that Jesus died for our offender's sins as well as our own and that the soul of this offender is just as precious to God as is our own.

"Once you were like sheep who wandered away. But now you have turned to your Shepherd, the Guardian of your souls." Without Jesus, we would be lost and without help. In forgiving, we follow a clear path that our Shepherd marks out for us; we can forgive freely and confidently because we know that our souls are safe.

You can take comfort in the fact that the passage outlined above was written by Peter. He was the disciple who three times denied Jesus on the night of His arrest. Peter was so devastated by his betrayal that, Scripture records, he "wept bitterly."[3] Yet when women visited Jesus' tomb after His burial and found it to be empty, an angel told them that Jesus had risen. "Go," the angel added, "tell his disciples *and Peter* [italics added]."[4] Peter was to know that Jesus still loved him and had forgiven him. Peter wrote the above passage for sinful yet forgiven followers of Jesus just like himself.

We know that we are unworthy to walk in Jesus' footsteps. Yet Scripture assures us that if we faithfully follow the paths He chooses for us, somewhere along the journey our footsteps will begin to match His.[5]

Today's Fitness Challenge - Day 4

☑ FEED YOUR SOUL: *"Let the same mind be in you that was in Christ Jesus."*

— Philippians 2:5 (NRSV)

☑ LISTEN TO FORGIVENESS: When I act on my decision to forgive, Christ's goodness becomes visible in me.

☑ CHECK YOUR HEART: What do I fear most about following in Christ's footsteps?

☑ KEEP GOING: With God's help, I will do good to those who have offended me.

Bonus Challenge

1. In what ways do I suffer the most from holding onto grudges? How could my forgiving help me?

2. What feelings motivate me to seek revenge? What do I hope my revenge will accomplish? How does human vengeance differ from God's vengeance, and why does He reserve that responsibility for Himself?

3. Has anyone ever loved me with a "covering" love that blotted out my offenses? What effects did such love have on me?

Week One
Day 5

Where Does It Hurt?

It is not enemies who taunt me –
I could bear that;
it is not adversaries who deal insolently with me –
I could hide from them.
But it is you, my equal,
my companion, my familiar friend,
with whom I kept pleasant company;
we walked in the house of God with the throng. (Psalm 55:12-
14, NRSV)

Forgiveness is always about people.

When we get hurt, we look for someone to blame. We point out the offensive behaviors that in some way damaged or insulted us. Affixing blame helps us to feel in control; we hope that, in knowing who was to blame for our hurt, we can protect ourselves from being hurt again.

As easy and reasonable as blaming seems, however, identifying the real source of our suffering can be difficult. The obvious offender linked with an obvious offense may be only the tip of a hidden iceberg. Seemingly offensive words or actions may touch on deeper layers of wounding within us, painful experiences from our past that have not healed and are still sensitive and easily triggered. We may have no conscious memory of these painful events from the past, or the memory we do have may be incomplete or distorted.

When an obvious offense stirs up emotions from an unobvious wound, forgiving becomes complicated. We may find it impossible to forgive what others might deem a minor offense. Or we do forgive but do not feel the relief from anger and pain that we expect.

The process of forgiving requires us to examine the offense itself, its depth and its nature, and determine who was responsible. Looking deeply into a wound may be unpleasant, sometimes so painful, in fact, that we try to satisfy ourselves with superficial blaming. If we are truly to forgive, however, we must know who it is we are forgiving and for what offense.

The Offense

Some offenses are as straightforward as they seem. A motorist swerves into your lane of traffic, cutting you off in a last-minute attempt to exit the freeway; teenagers crowd into the line ahead of you and get better seats in the theater; a hurrying passerby bumps your elbow and spills your coffee. These impersonal slights cause irritation, frustration, disappointment, perhaps even shock and anger. Even so, their effects are temporary and do not damage us at a deep level.

Not all offenses are so easy to identify or to dismiss. Offenses that cost us something — time, money, reputation, safety — stay with us longer and are more difficult to release: You wait all day for a repairman who never shows up and doesn't call; favoritism gets another employee promoted to the position you deserve. Moreover, as the cost to you increases, so does your resistance to forgiving: Your identity is stolen; arson fire ravages your neighborhood; your child is kidnapped on the way home from school.

Offenses that expose our vulnerabilities or threaten what we value are especially difficult to forgive. They tap into our fears and provoke instinctive defensive reactions. We are outraged; we are stricken with grief; we are confused and fearful. We want to see our offender punished and forced to compensate us for our losses. Sometimes we want pure, cold revenge.

Offenses are further complicated when they become personal, that is, when they are committed by someone we know and trust. *Betrayal* adds a layer of pain to any offense. It's bad enough to know that someone is spreading an ugly rumor about you; when that someone turns out to be your friend, the insult becomes a deep wound. Personal offenses are painful and difficult to release because they attack us at our roots. Our sense of safety in relationships is challenged when our trust is used against us. Infidelity, domestic violence, being cheated by a business associate, being robbed or lied to by a family member or close friend are betrayals so shattering that our *core beliefs—* how we make sense of the world and our place in it—are called into question. We may ask, *How can the God I believe in allow this to happen to me?*

Finally, offenses perpetrated during childhood have devastating, long-term consequences because they assault tender hearts and minds that are not yet fully formed. Children lack the maturity and experience to judge what is healthy or harmful in a relationship. Offenses need not be as blatant as physical or sexual abuse to have devastating effects; children who are repeatedly shamed, criticized, overlooked, exploited, deceived, or forced to witness domestic violence or the effects of substance abuse in those around them will grow up with inappropriate amounts of shame and guilt, a distorted concept of themselves, and misconceptions about what constitutes a normal, healthy relationship. Their core beliefs, including their concept of God and their own worthiness to be loved, can be severely compromised by such childhood wounding.

Overlapping Offenses

Sometimes we take offense where none is intended or overreact to a mild offense because someone's words or actions remind us of a previous, hurtful experience. We react to the present event *as if we are reacting to that past event*—we churn with old bitterness, pain, and fear; we see our old assailant in our new "offender"; we hear the old shaming message in the new words being spoken to us. We feel threatened, accused, ridiculed.

Old wounds that have never healed are powerful because we have made them part of our core belief system. Whether or not the words were actually spoken, we internalized messages that told us we were somehow lacking in what it takes to be acceptable or worthy of love. We currently misread situations and make incorrect assumptions about other people's motives because we are trying to make the world fit our core belief system, *even when that system causes us pain and despair*. We hear criticisms in neutral remarks because we *expect* to hear them; for example, when someone points out an error we've made, we immediately feel shame if somewhere along the way we internalized the message, "People who make mistakes are either lazy or stupid." We deflect sincere compliments and fight against the possibility that our belief system, which has somehow kept us going, could be wrong.

The Offender

Critical to forgiveness is determining who is really to blame for our wounding. Whom are we to forgive? As described above, we may blame someone in the present for unhealed anger and pain from our past. In other instances, we know who our offenders are but cannot bring ourselves to accuse them; instead, we blame other people, perhaps ourselves, or even God. This misdirected blaming is often unconscious. For example, abused children might condemn themselves for being flawed and deserving of their mistreatment rather than to believe that their parents do not love them; they grow up with little insight into why they are so angry and critical of themselves or why they feel distant from a cold and critical God. Likewise, victims of domestic violence or of spousal infidelity may blame themselves rather than their loved ones for the abuse and humiliations they suffer.

It is clear that forgiveness cannot take place until we have a concept of what is causing us pain and who is responsible. If we realize that we are, at least in part, responsible for our own suffering, then we must accept blame for our own actions and take steps to keep ourselves from repeating them. We may also owe apologies to those whom we have unfairly targeted with our anger and blame.

If we determine that others are responsible for offenses against us, then we must be careful and realistic in assigning damages. We must not blame someone in the present for damage that was done to us by someone else in the past. In naming both the wounds from our past and those who were responsible for them, we free our present relationships from the unfair burden of misdirected blaming. Forgiving the people in our lives now becomes easier, and we will have begun the important task of healing old wounds and forgiving those wounders as well.

Today's Fitness Challenge - Day 5

☑ FEED YOUR SOUL: *"Why is my pain unceasing, my wound incurable, refusing to be healed?"*

—Jeremiah 15:18 (NRSV)

☑ LISTEN TO FORGIVENESS: Old resentments are easily triggered by new events.

☑ CHECK YOUR HEART: What recent offense has been difficult for me to release?

☑ KEEP GOING: With God's help, I will recognize when I am angry with someone today because of a wound I suffered in the past.

Bonus Challenge

1. In what recent situation did I overreact to someone's words or actions? What was the offense, exactly, that triggered my response? How did I react? Whom did I hold responsible for the offense?

2. What is the deepest wound from my past that still haunts me today? Who was responsible for the wound? How would forgiving this person help me in my relationships today?

3. Name a recent offense that was easy to dismiss. What happened? Who was the offender? Why was this offense easy to release?

Week One
My Fitness Log

☑ *Complete each statement as found in the lesson indicated.* *

1. To forgive is to _____ on the decision to _____ and _____ _____ your offender. *(DAY 1)*

2. To the extent that I feel _____ and _____ by God, I can _____ and _____ others. *(DAY 1)*

3. When God asks you to forgive, He will _____ give you the _____ and the _____ to do it. *(DAY 2)*

4. God blesses me _____ when I share _____ _____ with others. *(DAY 2)*

5. Learning to forgive means learning to rely more and more on _____ _____ and less on _____ _____ _____. *(DAY 3)*

6. I make my own suffering _____ when I allow _____ _____ to take hold of my heart. *(DAY 3)*

7. For God called you to _____ _____, even if it means _____, just as Christ suffered for you. *(DAY 4)*

8. When I act on my _____ to forgive, Christ's goodness _____ _____ in me. *(DAY 4)*

9. Forgiveness is always about _____. *(DAY 5)*

10. Old _____ are easily triggered by _____ _____. *(DAY 5)*

* See Appendix A for answer key.

☑ Record the most important lesson you learned this week.

☑ Write a prayer to God. Tell Him truthfully what is in your heart at this stage of your walk and ask Him for what you need to continue.

Week One
Weekend Workout

Forgiveness Aptitude

THE WARM-UP. Read aloud from Psalm 139:

LORD, *you have examined me*
>*and know all about me.*
You know when I sit down and when I get up.
>*You know my thoughts before I think them.*
You know where I go and where I lie down.
>*You know thoroughly everything I do.*
LORD, *even before I say a word,*
>*you already know it.*
You are all around me — in front and in back —
>*and have put your hand on me.*
Your knowledge is amazing to me;
>*it is more than I can understand.*
Where can I go to get away from your Spirit?
>*Where can I run from you?*
If I go up to the heavens, you are there.
>*If I lie down in the grave, you are there.*
If I rise with the sun in the east
>*and settle in the west beyond the sea,*
even there you would guide me.
>*With your right hand you would hold me.*
I could say, "The darkness will hide me.
>*Let the light around me turn into night."*
But even the darkness is not dark to you.
>*The night is as light as the day;*

darkness and light are the same to you.
— *Psalm 139:1-12 (NCV)*

THE STRETCH. Read the psalm again, but this time silently and prayerfully. Ask the Holy Spirit to pray through the psalm with you.

Which words in particular capture your attention? Take a few moments now to meditate on them.

God knows you better than you know yourself — your mind, your history, your motives, your purpose in life. What in particular would you like to speak to Him about?

THE WORKOUT. As we travel down the road with forgiveness, it helps to realize that we are not the first to walk this way. Our Lord Jesus Christ walked it before us. He suffered insults and rejection and ultimately an agonizing death for sins that were not His own. In His complete obedience to the Father's will, He met every temptation with grace and strength, never retaliating, always returning good for evil. Even in His anger He did not sin but expressed godly indignation at the wickedness He encountered.[1] Because He was fully human as well as fully God, Jesus understands the sting in every wound that we suffer and our temptation to react out of anger and pain and thereby stumble into sin. The writer of Hebrews tells us, "For we do not have a high priest who is unable to sympathize with our weaknesses, but we have one who has been tempted in every way, just as we are — yet was without sin."[2] Jesus has already marked out the course for us. It only remains for us to follow Him as best we can.

Our readiness to forgive those who harm us can be called our *forgiveness aptitude*. When our anger and pain tempt us to sin, as they did Jesus, we can draw on spiritual resources for the strength and courage to follow God's way instead. These resources, or *forgiveness assets*, are our attitudes and beliefs and painful experiences that the Holy Spirit miraculously transforms into strengths as we submit ourselves in obedience to God. The more we empty ourselves before God, the more readily available these assets become. They are the resources we draw on to resist temptation and help us to forgive. They are the evidences that we belong to God.

The following inventory will help you to evaluate your aptitude for forgiving by examining your forgiveness assets. This inventory is not a test to determine whether you *can* forgive. Rather, it presents you with the opportunity to explore attitudes and habits that can either help you to forgive or cause you to stumble into sin. Directions for scoring and evaluating the inventory immediately follow the exercise.

Forgiveness Aptitude Inventory

Circle the answer that fits you the best. A good strategy is to answer quickly with the first answer that comes to your mind. Let your choices reflect how you really are and not how you think you should be. Use the following scoring method:

0	1	2	3
Not true	*Somewhat true*	*Mostly true*	*Very true*

0 1 2 3   1. God is the creator and sovereign Lord of everything in the world.

0 1 2 3   2. Mercy is more important than justice.

0 1 2 3   3. I tend to give people the benefit of the doubt.

0 1 2 3   4. Every day I try to be more like Christ.

0 1 2 3   5. I allow myself to feel angry or sad, but the feelings eventually pass.

0 1 2 3   6. I will never be good enough on my own to earn a place in God's kingdom.

0 1 2 3   7. Honesty is always the best policy.

0 1 2 3   8. No matter how bad things get, I always have choices.

0 1 2 3   9. God takes special delight in me.

0	1	2	3
Not true	*Somewhat true*	*Mostly true*	*Very true*

0 1 2 3 10. God has answered my prayers.

0 1 2 3 11. People deserve the bad things that happen to them.

0 1 2 3 12. I don't forgive, and I don't expect others to forgive me.

0 1 2 3 13. I am not good at making or keeping friends.

0 1 2 3 14. God loves others more than He loves me.

0 1 2 3 15. I enjoy the rush I get when I feel angry and powerful.

0 1 2 3 16. I react defensively when someone criticizes me.

0 1 2 3 17. I don't mind intimidating people when I know I'm right.

0 1 2 3 18. I am easily discouraged.

0 1 2 3 19. I am too ashamed to admit when I am wrong.

0 1 2 3 20. Worshipping God seldom touches me on a personal level.

0 1 2 3 21. Hurting others is wrong because it violates God's laws.

0 1 2 3 22. I always knew my family would love me no matter what I did.

0 1 2 3 23. I enjoy being with others, and I also enjoy being alone.

0	1	2	3
Not true	*Somewhat true*	*Mostly true*	*Very true*

0 1 2 3	24. I feel God's presence in my life.
0 1 2 3	25. I am careful in what I say to other people.
0 1 2 3	26. God is the source of everything good in my life.
0 1 2 3	27. I am always the same person no matter what situation I am in.
0 1 2 3	28. What I have suffered gives me special gifts for helping others.
0 1 2 3	29. I am comfortable with making mistakes.
0 1 2 3	30. I feel close to God in nature.
0 1 2 3	31. The presence of evil in the world is proof that God is not in control.
0 1 2 3	32. I pride myself on being a perfectionist.
0 1 2 3	33. If others knew who I really am, they would not like me.
0 1 2 3	34. God is distant, judging, and frankly unlikable.
0 1 2 3	35. My being sick or depressed gets me out of my responsibilities.
0 1 2 3	36. I feel compelled to share my opinion whether or not others ask for it.
0 1 2 3	37. It's okay to cheat as long as I don't hurt anyone.
0 1 2 3	38. Life makes no sense to me.

0	1	2	3
Not true	*Somewhat true*	*Mostly true*	*Very true*

0 1 2 3 39. I am damaged goods.

0 1 2 3 40. I have no sense of God working in my life.

0 1 2 3 41. God cares about my enemies as much as He cares about me.

0 1 2 3 42. I notice when others are suffering, and I want to help them.

0 1 2 3 43. I have built-in needs for relationship.

0 1 2 3 44. I show my love for God by loving other people.

0 1 2 3 45. I am not one to hold a grudge.

0 1 2 3 46. I readily apologize when I realize that I have been wrong.

0 1 2 3 47. I refuse to pass along rumors about people even when I think the rumors are true.

0 1 2 3 48. At least one person loved and believed in me when I was growing up.

0 1 2 3 49. I have no qualms about saying No to people.

0 1 2 3 50. I pray, fast, meditate, or study the Bible to get closer to God.

0 1 2 3 51. Once I have been saved by Jesus, I am free to behave any way I want.

0 1 2 3 52. Compassion clouds my judgment and keeps me from doing what's necessary.

0	1	2	3
Not true	*Somewhat true*	*Mostly true*	*Very true*

0 1 2 3   53. Strong people meet their own needs without relying on others.

0 1 2 3   54. I cannot forgive God for letting me down.

0 1 2 3   55. Crying makes me uncomfortable, whether it's my crying or someone else's.

0 1 2 3   56. I am a master at one-upmanship.

0 1 2 3   57. It is pointless to feel remorse over something that cannot be changed.

0 1 2 3   58. I cannot imagine living a different life.

0 1 2 3   59. I have thought about harming myself.

0 1 2 3   60. Praying to God doesn't work for me.

0 1 2 3   61. Satan is a real and powerful source of evil in our world.

0 1 2 3   62. I enjoy serving the needs of others.

0 1 2 3   63. People often ask me for help.

0 1 2 3   64. I am God's person.

0 1 2 3   65. It's okay to be angry at someone I love.

0 1 2 3   66. I am good at seeing things from another person's point of view.

0 1 2 3   67. I make promises carefully, and I always keep them.

0 1 2 3   68. I am confident that I will spend eternity with God.

0	1	2	3
Not true	*Somewhat true*	*Mostly true*	*Very true*

0 1 2 3   69. I take care of my body by eating well and exercising regularly.

0 1 2 3   70. I confess my sins and ask God to forgive me.

0 1 2 3   71. Truth is relative, defined by time and culture.

0 1 2 3   72. People suffer afflictions because God is punishing them.

0 1 2 3   73. People will take advantage of me if they get the chance.

0 1 2 3   74. I cannot love a God who won't protect innocent people from being hurt.

0 1 2 3   75. I have a hard time identifying my feelings.

0 1 2 3   76. I have been described as boastful.

0 1 2 3   77. I misrepresent myself to others because I want them to accept me.

0 1 2 3   78. I don't trust myself to make the right choices.

0 1 2 3   79. I learned to hide my real self from others when I was growing up.

0 1 2 3   80. I have little interest in reading the Bible.

Scoring and Evaluating My Inventory Answers

<u>Step 1:</u> GROUP I SCORES. Transfer to the table below your answers for inventory statement numbers 1-10, 21-30, 41-50, and 61-70. Add across each row and record the totals.

Group I Scores				Group I Totals	Forgiveness Asset
1:	21:	41:	61:		Christian Worldview
2:	22:	42:	62:		Compassion
3:	23:	43:	63:		Connectedness
4:	24:	44:	64:		Devotion to God
5:	25:	45:	65:		Emotional Discipline
6:	26:	46:	66:		Humility
7:	27:	47:	67:		Integrity
8:	28:	48:	68:		Resilience
9:	29:	49:	69:		Self-Acceptance
10:	30:	50:	70:		Spiritual Practice

<u>Step 2:</u> GROUP II SCORES. Transfer to the table below your answers for inventory statement numbers 11-20, 31-40, 51-60, and 71-80. Add across each row and record the totals.

Group II Scores				Group II Totals	Forgiveness Asset
11:	31:	51:	71:		Christian Worldview
12:	32:	52:	72:		Compassion

13:	33:	53:	73:		Connectedness
14:	34:	54:	74:		Devotion to God
15:	35:	55:	75:		Emotional Discipline
16:	36:	56:	76:		Humility
17:	37:	57:	77:		Integrity
18:	38:	58:	78:		Resilience
19:	39:	59:	79:		Self-Acceptance
20:	40:	60:	80:		Spiritual Practice

Step 3: Complete the table below by subtracting Group II totals from Group I totals, and recording the difference for each Asset row.

Group I Total – Group II Total = Asset Score	Forgiveness Asset
_____ – _____ = _____	Christian Worldview
_____ – _____ = _____	Compassion
_____ – _____ = _____	Connectedness
_____ – _____ = _____	Devotion to God
_____ – _____ = _____	Emotional Discipline
_____ – _____ = _____	Humility
_____ – _____ = _____	Integrity
_____ – _____ = _____	Resilience
_____ – _____ = _____	Self-Acceptance

_____ - _____ = _____	Spiritual Practice

Note: If the Group II total is larger than the Group I total, the Asset Score will be negative. For example, if the Group I score is 2 and the Group II score is 6, the Asset Score will be -4.

Step 4: Plot your Asset Scores on the graph below. A sample graph is shown on the following page.

My Forgiveness Aptitude

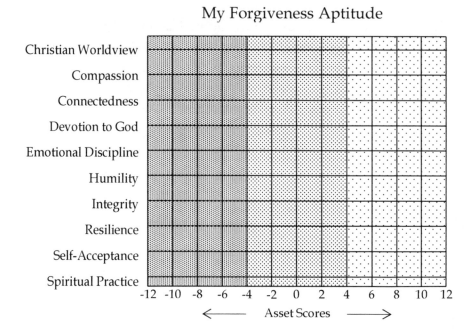

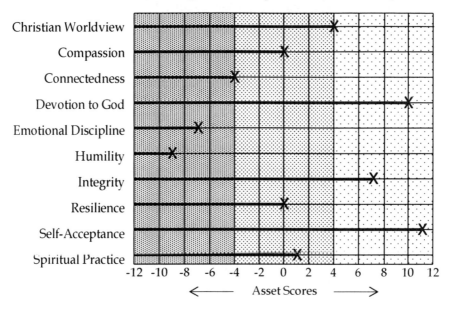

Forgiveness Aptitude (SAMPLE)

Note: A higher score suggests more readiness to forgive. A lower score indicates less readiness and the opportunity to grow toward forgiveness.

<u>Step 5</u>: Record your Asset Score for each of the categories listed below. Read the descriptions and consider how each asset affects your readiness to forgive.

<u>My Score</u>   <u>Asset Category</u>

_____   **Christian Worldview.** What we believe filters our experiences and shapes our attitudes and decisions. A Christian's worldview is rooted in the belief that God is the creator and sustainer of the universe, that the Bible is God's own revelation to us, that Christ died a sinless death for our sins and rose again, and that we should follow His example in making life choices. *How does my Christian worldview help me to forgive?*

Compassion. To feel compassion for others is to recognize when they are in some way suffering and to want to help them. Receiving love and mercy from others, including God, teaches and motivates us to extend the same to others. *How does my compassion help me to forgive?*

Connectedness. People who are mentally healthy enjoy being connected with others through relationships. Good boundaries help us to connect safely with others and balance our need for solitude. Although God designed us to seek out relationships, we must learn the social skills necessary for relating to each other in healthy ways. *How does my connectedness help me to forgive?*

Devotion to God. God designed us not only for relationship with each other but especially for relationship with Himself. Our devotion to God is our pressing desire to be in His presence, to learn His ways and follow them, to celebrate His greatness, to praise and thank Him for His many blessings, and to share our love and knowledge of Him with others. *How does my devotion to God help me to forgive?*

Emotional Discipline. Feelings are important, but

they can lead us down the wrong paths when they are out of control. When we are emotionally disciplined, we recognize and accept our feelings but do not let them dictate our attitudes and behaviors. *How does my emotional discipline help me to forgive?*

_____ **Humility**. To be humble is the opposite of being proud; to act with humility is to set aside our self-centeredness and to act in the best interests of others. We are humble when we treat others with respect and recognize our own sinfulness. *How does my humility help me to forgive?*

_____ **Integrity**. Biblical integrity implies wholeness, uprightness, and honesty of character. Our spiritual integrity is a gift from God, who declares us to be whole and without blemish because of Christ's sacrifice. We act with integrity when we obey God's laws and reflect to others His holy perfection. *How does my integrity help me to forgive?*

_____ **Resilience**. People with resilience are not crushed by trauma or hardships but find ways to recover and go on with their lives. Resilient people are characterized by their confidence that they can make the future better, that they have choices, and that there is always hope. *How does my resilience help me to forgive?*

_____ **Self-Acceptance**. Those who truly accept themselves know their worth. The shame and guilt they experience are corrective but not demoralizing.

They are not afraid to see themselves as they truly are or to let others see them as well. They know they are sinful, yet they also feel accepted and loved by God. *How does my self-acceptance help me to forgive?*

_____ **Spiritual Practice**. Through spiritual practices, we open our lives to God: we experience His presence, hear His voice, express our hearts to Him, and go deeper into a knowledge of Him and what it means to follow Him. Some of these practices are prayer, meditation, worship, fasting, study, confession, silence, celebration, and service. *How does my spiritual practice help me to forgive?*

THE COOL-DOWN. Take a few moments to reflect on your highest and lowest Asset Scores. Were you surprised by any of the results? Which inventory statements did you struggle to answer? Go back now and mark them for future consideration. Appendix B lists the statements in groups under each asset category so that you can consider each asset separately.

As you continue your walk with forgiveness in the remaining weeks, look for references to your asset strengths in the reading material. Ask God to show you what He particularly has to teach *you* in each lesson.

Close the session by praying the last two verses of Psalm 139:

> *Search me, O God, and know my heart;*
> > *test me and know my anxious thoughts.*
> *Point out anything in me that offends you,*
> > *and lead me along the path of everlasting life. (NLT)*

PART TWO

Practicing Forgiveness

Trust God from the bottom of your heart; don't try to figure out
everything on your own.
Listen for God's voice in everything you do, everywhere you go; he's
the one who will keep you on track.

Proverbs 3:5-6, MSG

Week Two

Come, let us go up to the mountain of the LORD,
to the house of the God of Jacob.
He will teach us his ways,
so that we may walk in his paths. (Isaiah 2:3)

Week Two
Day 1

Begin with God

One of them, a lawyer, spoke up: "Sir, which is the most important command in the laws of Moses?" Jesus replied, "'Love the Lord your God with all your heart, soul, and mind.' This is the first and greatest commandment. The second most important is similar: 'Love your neighbor as much as you love yourself.' All the other commandments and all the demands of the prophets stem from these two laws and are fulfilled if you obey them. Keep only these and you will find that you are obeying all the others." (Matthew 22:35–40, TLB)

More important than forgiving is learning to love God.

Love for God is the foundation for the Christian walk. It is the key to joyful obedience and the answer to the human quest for meaning. Learning to love God is the most important and profound task upon which we can set our minds. It is the ultimate tonic for our hearts, which were crafted to receive love and to respond in kind. It is the fulfillment of our soul's yearning for home and for the One whose arms wait for us.

In the Matthew passage quoted above, a legal expert approached Jesus to test His knowledge of Jewish law. This lawyer spoke for the Pharisees, who of all Jews were particularly proud of knowing and keeping all the religious rules described in the Book of Moses. Perhaps this lawyer expected Jesus to reply with a rule about conduct, such as "Do not murder" or "Do not make for yourself an idol." Jesus, however, responded by quoting two commandments that speak more to the "why" than the "what" of Jewish religion. Love, He reminded them, is the key. If you want your noble acts and sacrifices to please God, then make sure they are motivated by love.

Such a pronouncement insulted the Pharisees, whom Jesus elsewhere accused of being "whitewashed tombs," appearing righteous on the outside but inside being full of hypocrisy and wickedness.[1] He denounced their rigid adherence to God's laws as meaningless because their love for God Himself had been forgotten.

Jesus took the first commandment—to love God with all your heart, soul, and mind—from an Old Testament passage.[2] This excerpt from Deuteronomy was so important that it became the *Shema*, a confession of faith that pious Jews prayed regularly, yet its essential meaning had been lost. The second commandment—to love your neighbor as yourself—He also took from the Old Testament.[3] Both passages speak to the spirit of love underlying every law that Jews were bound to obey. Moreover, Jesus declared that a righteous life will flow *automatically* from the observance of just these two commandments.

But how do we love God with *all* our heart, *all* our soul, *all* our mind? Quickly, we see that keeping this first commandment is far more difficult than keeping rules about what to eat or how to prepare a temple sacrifice. It challenges us to change *internally*, to realign our desires, our feelings, our very thoughts in ways that are pleasing to God. This process is, in fact, the holiness we seek as Christians. It is an ongoing refinement that makes us fit for eternal fellowship with our Creator and the Lover of our souls.

The second commandment Jesus called similar to the first, and it flows from the first. As the apostle John reminds us, all love begins with God, and we cannot love each other if we do not know and love God first. Conversely, if we love God, then we must also love each other.[4] We love our neighbors with the very love that God gives us and with a heart that He is refining in us as we learn to love Him better.

An often neglected part of the second commandment is to love your neighbor "as much as you love yourself." It is not a sin to love yourself; in fact, this commandment implies that it is a sin *not* to love yourself. The passage is not talking about self-aggrandizing or narcissism, which are rooted in shame and pride, but rather a healthy appreciation of yourself as a reflection of God's own image and the precious object of His love.

Each of the Ten Commandments and their associated tenets can be understood as an expression of at least one of these three kinds of love: love of God, love of neighbor, and love of self. "You shall not make for yourself an idol,"[5] for example, is about loving God; "You shall not murder"[6] is about loving your neighbor. "You shall not give false testimony against your neighbor"[7] is about loving your neighbor and also about loving yourself well enough to keep your moral integrity intact.

Jesus added a final touch to the second commandment by stretching the concept of neighbor: "Love your enemies and pray for those who persecute you."[8] What can this teaching mean to us? The stranger who covets and takes what is yours, the coworker who gossips about you, the spouse who cheats on you, the parent who rejects you, the child who lies to you, the friend who betrays you—all are your "neighbors." You are to love them not because they are particularly lovable but because you know and love God, and *He* loves them, as completely and as extravagantly as He loves you. Loving your neighbors thus becomes an expression of your love for God and forgiving them an act of worship.

Today's Fitness Challenge - Day 1

☑ FEED YOUR SOUL: *"A man's spiritual health is exactly proportional to his love for God."*

—C.S. Lewis, author

☑ LISTEN TO FORGIVENESS: Learning to love God helps me to love and forgive my neighbor.

☑ CHECK YOUR HEART: Do I have more difficulty loving God, my neighbor, or myself?

☑ KEEP GOING: With God's help, I will focus my attention less on how I've been wounded and more on how I can deepen my love for God.

Bonus Challenge

1. Is it possible to forgive without love? Have I ever tried it? What does loveless forgiveness look like? How does it differ from forgiveness that is rooted in love?

2. Is it easier for me to forgive a stranger or someone close to me? Why?

3. Why is God so concerned with our loving our neighbors? Who benefits most when we love and forgive each other? Who is hurt when we refuse to love or forgive?

Week Two
Day 2

The Cross at the Crossroad

Today I have set before you life or death, blessing or curse. Oh, that you would choose life; that you and your children might live! Choose to love the Lord your God and to obey him and to cling to him, for he is your life and the length of your days. (Deuteronomy 30:19-20, TLB)

Every wounding experience places you at a new crossroad.

A crossroad is a critical point on our walk where the path ahead diverges, and we must decide which way to go. Life events such as marriage, a job transfer, or the birth of a child commonly position us at junctures where we must consider new paths to follow. We choose one path over another based upon what we know about ourselves and our resources and what sort of destination we have in mind. We will consider which paths are more attractive, more difficult, or more costly. We decide what we are willing to sacrifice in order to follow a particular path.

A wounding event also positions us at an important life juncture. Whether a personal betrayal, a professional injustice, or a random act of cruelty, the wound becomes critical as we realize that the path ahead cannot be the same as the one we have been traveling. Like it or not, our future will be different from the one we had planned. Life is forcing us to make a choice.

How will we respond to the person who hurt us? Which path will we choose? And how will that choice affect our future?

In Christ we have a perfect model of how to respond to wounding events. He was wounded in every significant way:

beaten	robbed of life	targeted
falsely accused	shackled	tempted
misunderstood	isolated	disfigured
abandoned	disfavored	hated
betrayed	scapegoated	dismissed
outcast	rejected	maligned
humiliated	criticized	suspected
overpowered	ridiculed	
physically violated	overlooked	

Despite the injustice of His wounding, Christ did not choose the way of the world but chose to follow the course that God had set for Him, even to death on the cross. He not only forgave His tormentors but also begged His Father to forgive them[1]. He took on sins that were not His own and sacrificed His life purely out of love. He triumphed over His wounds by trusting God's faithfulness, and God raised Him to glory.

When you are wounded by another, your first response will likely be emotional—anger, hurt, disappointment, incredulity, sorrow. The shock of the wound causes an energy surge that can cloud your judgment and distort thought processes. As you experience your emotions, however, they will discharge some of that energy, and eventually you will be able to once again think rationally. You will find yourself at a crossroad with two choices facing you.

You can listen to the recommendations of the world and choose a course of blame, self-interest, and revenge. The apostle Paul describes companions who wait for you on this path, among them hatred, discord, jealousy, fits of rage, selfish ambition, and envy[2]. Such companions hold forgiveness in contempt and scoff at the notion of surrendering your bargaining power by reconciling with the person who hurt you.

When you remember the cross, however, you can choose to follow instead the course that Jesus took. You can release judgment and punishment to God and free your heart to love and to forgive what the world tells you is unlovable and unforgivable. Grace and mercy will walk with you, along with joy, peace, patience, kindness, goodness, faithfulness, gentleness, and self-control[3].

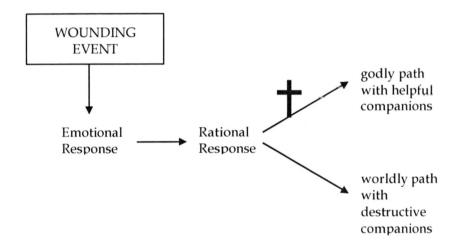

Today's Fitness Challenge - Day 2

☑ FEED YOUR SOUL: *"Every day the choice between good and evil is presented to us in simple ways."*
— William Edwyn Robert Sangster, Methodist minister

☑ LISTEN TO FORGIVENESS: Christ's sacrifice on the cross reminds me that I *always* have the choice to forgive.

☑ CHECK YOUR HEART: How is my wound similar to what Jesus suffered?

☑ KEEP GOING: With God's help, I will recognize when I am at a crossroad and will remember the choice that Christ made on my behalf.

Bonus Challenge

1. When have I come to a relationship crossroad and chosen the worldly path? What were the consequences of that decision?

2. Have I suffered a wound that is not on the list of Christ's wounds? If so, do I believe that this wound puts me beyond God's expectation that I should forgive?

3. What could have tempted Jesus to forsake the path leading to the cross and to take the worldly path? What convinced Him to stay the course God had chosen for Him?

Week Two
Day 3

Meet the Enemy

Submit yourselves therefore to God. Resist the devil, and he will flee from you. Draw near to God, and he will draw near to you. Cleanse your hands, you sinners, and purify your hearts, you double-minded. (James 4:7–8, NRSV)

Your Enemy is not the person who hurt you.

There is no doubt that our human enemies cause us to suffer. They betray our trust, take what we treasure, malign our reputation. They damage us financially, socially, physically, and psychologically. They shatter our defenses and lead us to doubt whether justice will ever prevail.

Nevertheless, the Bible warns us that our true threat lies not in our human enemies (small "e") but in Satan, our true Enemy (capital "E"), whom the apostle Paul calls "the mighty prince of the power of the air, who is at work right now in the hearts of those who are against the Lord."[1] Our true Enemy, also called the devil, is the essence of evil, consumed with hatred for God and bent on corrupting whatever belongs to God. He is the opposite of God; while God desires nothing but our good, "not wanting anyone to perish, but everyone to come to repentance,"[2] Satan craves our eternal destruction and the defeat of God in this world.

Without God to help us, we are powerless to escape the snares of this Enemy. In the Scripture quotation from James above, people are described as being double-minded, that is, pulled both toward God and toward Satan. Because we are each made in the image of God, we have a nature that responds to God and is attracted to goodness. Even without God's sanctifying grace, we can make moral choices and accomplish great things in the name of goodness. These good deeds won't save us, yet they reflect our instinct to choose what is right, what is just, what is generous. Also within us, however, and battling for our attention is our sinful nature. This is the side of us that finds Satan and sin attractive. This nature leads us away from God and into selfish behaviors and choices that damage our relationships, hurt us physically and emotionally, and destroy our peace.

Our divided loyalties place us on a continuum between goodness and evil, or between God and Satan, as shown in the diagram below. In our double-mindedness we are attracted to God's goodness but also to sin and wickedness. Resisting sin moves us closer to God; embracing sin moves us away from Him and closer to our Enemy.

As humans, we all share this "+/-" duality. The apostle Paul described this internal conflict in Christians as our sin nature warring with the Spirit of God in us and keeping us from doing what we know is right.[3] Every day we find ourselves moving to the left and to the right, pulled like pins between the magnetic poles of good and evil.

But we are not the evil. People who hurt us may do evil things, but they are not the evil, either. The evil we dread is our Enemy, the One who teases and whispers and tantalizes us with those particular sins he knows we cannot resist. Satan is without mercy in his efforts to bring us to ruin. Even when we have accepted Christ's sacrifice on the cross and have been covered with God's mercy, the Enemy knows he can still attract us and use us for his own dark purposes.

As we follow our sinful desires deeper into Satan's territory, it is as if we ourselves become magnetized and begin to attract others with our sin. Our selfish choices and lifestyles offer free advertising for evil as we work to make our sin look as attractive, as pleasurable, as *harmless* as possible. As misery loves company, so does sin. People hide from those pleasure-spoilers—guilt and shame—by persuading others to come alongside and enjoy their sin with them. Meanwhile, the Father of Lies sits back and applauds.

Fortunately, while the Enemy is hard at work trapping and tricking and luring people to wickedness, God is fighting for our souls with a powerful weapon that Satan does not have and has never understood—*love*. God never stops wooing us to life in the kingdom and eternal relationship with Him. When we accept God's love into our hearts, we in turn can extend this love to others and thus become magnetized for *goodness*. God uses our every act of obedience to neutralize Satan's allure and turn people's attention toward heaven.

That we should forgive our enemies is important to God because He longs for the restoration of every human soul. And nothing attracts a soul toward God more powerfully than a genuine act of love. Scripture describes behaviors that make such love unmistakable:

Love your enemies, do good to those who hate you, bless those who curse you, pray for those who mistreat you. If someone strikes you on one cheek, turn to him the other also. If someone takes your cloak, do not stop him from taking your tunic. Give to everyone who asks you, and if anyone takes what belongs to you, do not demand it back. Do to others as you would have them do to you.[4]

If your enemy is hungry, feed him; if he is thirsty, give him something to drink.[5]

Do not gloat when your enemy falls; when he stumbles, do not let your heart rejoice.[6]

God's first desire is not to punish the world but to redeem the lost. Satan, the Enemy, the self-declared hater of God, has already put himself beyond redemption. God's condemnation of him is sealed. But God has not given up on us: "When we were utterly helpless with no way of escape, Christ came at just the right time and died for us sinners who had no use for him."[7] Human enemies of God become friends of God through the transforming power of His love and mercy. We are to follow God's example, forgiving and loving our enemies, because God, with tender and profound grace, loved and forgave us first.

Today's Fitness Challenge - Day 3

☑ FEED YOUR SOUL: *"Be self-controlled and alert. Your enemy the devil prowls around like a roaring lion looking for someone to devour."*

—1 Peter 5:8

☑ LISTEN TO FORGIVENESS: Choosing to forgive moves me toward God and magnetizes me for goodness.

☑ CHECK YOUR HEART: When someone offends me, how does my response pull me to the right or to the left?

☑ KEEP GOING: With God's help, I will recognize my true Enemy in Satan and not in double-minded humans like myself.

Bonus Challenge

1. Is there someone whom I consider to be my enemy? In what specific ways do I think this person has sinned against me? Have I ever sinned or been tempted to sin in the same or similar ways?

2. How does God expect me to love my enemies and show kindness to those who have hurt me? Has anyone ever shown love and kindness to me after I had indulged in hurtful behavior? Why would that person treat me in such a generous way?

3. Who in my life has acted like a magnet for wickedness? How did Satan use this person to tempt me away from God? In

what ways has Satan used me like a magnet to tempt others into sin? Do I need to apologize to anyone and ask for forgiveness?

Week Two
Day 4

Forgiving the Penitent

The son said to him, "Father, I have sinned against heaven and against you. I am no longer worthy to be called your son." But the father said to his servants, "Quick! Bring the best robe and put it on him. Put a ring on his finger and sandals on his feet. Bring the fattened calf and kill it. Let's have a feast and celebrate. For this son of mine was dead and is alive again; he was lost and is found." So they began to celebrate. (Luke 15:21-24)

Godly forgiveness is spontaneous, nonjudgmental, restorative, joyful, and rooted in love.

Luke 15:11-32 recounts a story told by Jesus that we know as the Parable of the Lost or Prodigal Son. The longest parable recorded, this story is important because it gives us a vivid picture of how God the Father forgives and welcomes a lost soul who turns from sin. It also gives us a realistic picture of what stands in the way of our accepting His forgiveness or forgiving each other.

Jesus was speaking to a crowd that included Pharisees and teachers of the law who had been grumbling about the sordid company He was keeping. To answer their objections, Jesus told them a story about a young Jew who insults his father by demanding an early inheritance and then rejects and disgraces his family by running off to a foreign land and squandering his inheritance on "wild living." Furthermore, when a famine hits the land, he takes a job slopping pigs, the most despicable job imaginable for a Jew who considers pigs to be unclean animals. Thoroughly humiliated, hungry, alone, and desperate, the son decides to return home and throw himself upon the mercy of his father.

As we read in the excerpt quoted above, the son humbles himself before his father. He names his offenses and confesses his unworthiness to expect mercy. Yet he knows that mercy is what he needs; if his father rejects him, he is doomed. The son is prepared to beg his father to hire him as a servant in the very household where he had previously ranked as the legitimate son of a wealthy landowner. His humbling is indeed profound.

We can look for lessons about forgiveness in the different ways that the characters in the story respond to this wayward son's homecoming.

The Father

Surely the crowds listening to Jesus were as amazed as we are today at the extravagant show of love and forgiveness that this father poured out upon his son! Jesus clearly intended that the father in the story should illustrate for us the generous nature of our Father in heaven, who welcomes with great rejoicing the lost soul who repents and seeks His mercy. In the father's response to his son, we recognize five important characteristics of godly forgiveness:

Forgiveness is spontaneous. The parable tells us: "But while [the son] was still a long way off, his father saw him and was filled with compassion for him; he ran to his son, threw his arms around him and kissed him." The mere sight of his son's returning was enough to compel this father to action. Without hesitation, heedless of appearances, he hiked up his robes and ran straight out to meet his son, embraced him, and kissed him.

Forgiveness is nonjudgmental. We are not told whether the father had any notion of what his son had been doing during the long period of his absence. Regardless, the father required no explanation or apology. The son did not utter a word before his father threw his arms around him and gave him a welcoming kiss. The fact that his son had returned was enough to satisfy this father.

Forgiveness is restorative. The son never got the chance to ask his father to take him back as a servant. Instead, his father immediately told the servants to bring his son a robe, a ring, and sandals for his feet as an immediate show of honor: sandals and robes were worn by family members and important guests; the ring was probably a signet ring of authority. The father was making it clear to everyone that he was restoring his son to the position he had always held in the family. There was to be no trial period in which the son would have to prove himself worthy.

Forgiveness is joyful. The father's joy over his son's return was extravagant and unprecedented. After their emotional reunion, the father ordered the fattened calf to be killed and prepared for a celebration feast; he called in people to celebrate with him with music and dancing: "For this son of mine was dead and is alive again; he was lost and is found." The father celebrated without reserve the restoration of the beloved child who had been lost to him.

Forgiveness is rooted in love. The story tells us that at the first sight of his son, the father was filled with compassion. Love motivated everything the father subsequently did: running out to meet his son, embracing and kissing him, covering his ragged clothes and dirty feet, and publicly acknowledging the restoration of his son with a signet ring and a celebration party. The son's relationship with the father was restored not because he in any way deserved it but because the father loved him so deeply and completely that he had no other desire than to show his son mercy.

The Older Brother

The second half of the parable (verses 25-32) introduces the older brother. He returns from working in the field to discover that his wastrel younger brother has come home, safe and sound. Not only that, but their father has killed the precious fattened calf to celebrate, and a party is now in full swing. The loving mercy of the father's heart is emphasized all the more by contrasting it with the unloving and unforgiving attitude of this older brother.

Unforgiveness is rigid. When the older brother heard the news that his younger brother had returned, he "became angry and refused to go in [to the celebration]." Without speaking to his brother or learning the circumstances of his return, the older brother nevertheless took a rigid posture of stubborn rejection.

Unforgiveness is judgmental. When the father went out to urge the older brother to come inside and celebrate with them, his son retorted: "Look! All these years I've been slaving for you and never disobeyed your orders. Yet you never gave me even a young goat so I could celebrate with my friends. But when this son of yours who has squandered your property with prostitutes comes home, you kill the fattened calf for him!" The older brother criticized his father for what he deemed a lavish and unwarranted display of love and welcome for a worthless son. Moreover, he held himself up as the measure of a good son who always did things right and who merited his father's favor more than the ne'er-do-well younger son.

Unforgiveness is distancing. The older son was not interested in restoring a relationship with his brother. He emphasized this point when he referred to the younger brother as "this son of yours" rather than as his own brother. At the end of the story, the father gently reminded the older brother of his relationship when he said, *"This brother of yours* was dead and is alive again; he was lost and is found" (italics added).

Unforgiveness is resentful. The return of the younger son stirred up bitterness in the older brother that had been brewing for a long time. Not only did he resent the younger brother's warm reception, but he also resented his father's refusal to acknowledge his own importance as the more worthy son. Because of his years of service, he felt entitled to his father's special favor and indulgence.

Unforgiveness is rooted in expectations. The older brother was angry because, according to his rule book, he merited his father's gratitude and admiration but did not receive them. Although he had lived with his father all his life, his service was based upon duty rather than love. Honor, obedience, and filial obligation were the standards by which he judged himself to be a good son, and his brother to be a bad son. Mercy that was not merited — the essence of forgiveness — was beyond his comprehension.

As clearly as the father of the story illustrates the nature of God the Father welcoming lost sinners, the older brother illustrates the hearts of the Pharisees, who considered themselves to be close to God not because of love but because of their careful observance of religious rules and outward appearances of piety. The parable ends without telling us what the older brother decided to do about his brother's return. Likewise, the Pharisees had the choice to adopt the father's attitude toward repentant sinners or to persist in their illusion of righteous superiority. Like the older brother, until they could see themselves as desperate sinners in need of unmerited mercy like the younger brother, they could not appreciate the character and depth of the father's forgiveness.

We, too, have a choice to make. God invites us to celebrate

with Him the return of all who realize their sin and repent, no matter how wicked their deeds, and not to stand on the outside, pouting and refusing to enter. If we wish to be godly forgivers, then we must stop relying on our personal goodness and confess our guilt and our need for God's mercy. Further, we must recognize *ourselves* in the sins of those who offend us and forgive them as joyfully and completely as God forgives us.

Today's Fitness Challenge - Day 4

☑ FEED YOUR SOUL: *"He who conceals his sins does not prosper, but whoever confesses and renounces them finds mercy."*
— Proverbs 28:13

☑ LISTEN TO FORGIVENESS: Mercy is a gift, not a reward.

☑ CHECK YOUR HEART: Am I more like the father, the older brother, or the younger brother in this parable?

☑ KEEP GOING: With God's help, I will confess my unrighteousness and throw myself upon the mercy of the Father.

Bonus Challenge

1. In what ways do I try to merit God's forgiveness? Has there been a time when I believed that I was more deserving of God's mercy than someone else because my sins were less reprehensible?

2. How am I like or unlike the father in the parable? What would I have to change in my life to become more like him?

3. How would I feel about God's throwing a party to celebrate His love for my offender? Would I accept His invitation to rejoice with Him, or would I remain outside?

Week Two
Day 5

How Much Is Enough?

Keep your conscience clear, so that, when you are maligned, those who abuse you for your good conduct in Christ may be put to shame. For it is better to suffer for doing good, if suffering should be God's will, than to suffer for doing evil. (1 Peter 3:16–18, NRSV)

Pain is the currency you use to meet the cost of refusing to forgive.

Anyone who has burned a hand on a hot stove or pounded a finger instead of a nail knows the power of pain. Nothing gets our attention more quickly or more thoroughly. Pain is our built-in alarm system that sounds off when something is wrong. It warns us that a boundary has been violated and that a change in strategy is immediately called for to prevent further injury.

Physical pain is the clearest example of how the pain system works. Nerve endings interpret signals such as pressure or heat as dangerous, and we respond reflexively and evasively: we snatch our hand away from the hot stove; we drop the nail. Human pain response is, in fact, so sophisticated that the spinal cord gives the order for evasive action even before the nerve signal reaches the brain and registers as *pain*.

In addition to physical pain, we also suffer emotional, social, and mental pain. Being robbed at gunpoint, watching a loved one die, receiving a diagnosis of serious illness, discovering a spouse's infidelity, losing a job, suffering public humiliation—our minds interpret such experiences as traumatic pain. Such pain can feel as real and severe as physical pain and similarly motivates us to alter our behavior. We become nervous, aggressive, depressed, or suspicious. We change our routines and avoid certain people or situations. We take more safety precautions but still don't feel safe. We question our belief system, our values, our faith in God. We look in the mirror and wonder if our lives can ever return to normal.

We also fear pain that might occur in the future. We anticipate the *potential* for harm and barricade ourselves behind a wall of behaviors we hope will protect us. Phobia is a clinical example of this anticipatory fear, but such fear is common in everyday relationships as well. When someone we trust hurts us, we fear being hurt again. We examine our vulnerabilities and shore up our defenses to avoid more pain. Unfortunately, our defensive strategies may inflict far more pain on us than the anticipated pain we are hoping to avoid.

Withholding forgiveness is a common defensive strategy for responding to relationship pain, yet it comes at a high cost. Far from relieving pain, a rigid, resentful stance tends to generate pain of its own, thus adding another layer of suffering. We succeed only in making a hurtful situation worse. Examples of the pain we cause ourselves by refusing to forgive are described in List A below.

List A: *Pain I cause myself by refusing to forgive...*
___ I am angry all the time.
___ My thoughts are trapped in ruminations about my injury.
___ I do not sleep well.
___ I cannot allow myself to grieve my lost relationship, *or* I am grieving all the time.
___ I withdraw into myself.
___ My life feels stuck in the wounding experience.
___ Bitterness and sorrow overshadow my efforts to be happy.

___ I feel compelled to say malicious things about the person who hurt me.

___ I am disappointed in God.

___ I am angry at myself for being so vulnerable.

___ I spend too much energy on trying to figure out why this happened to me.

___ My body is paying a price with headaches, stomach aches, fatigue, neck pain, etc.

___ My prayer life is ineffective; I feel distant from God and my faith.

___ My other relationships suffer because I am so angry, depressed, and/or anxious.

We pay for the luxury of refusing to forgive by suffering these various pains and others not listed. Take a look at List B below and see if your reasons for withholding forgiveness justify the price you pay in suffering.

List B: *My reasons for refusing to forgive...*

___ I'm waiting for an apology.

___ I must punish the person who hurt me.

___ My trust was betrayed.

___ I don't want others to think I am passive or weak.

___ I didn't deserve what happened to me.

___ My wounder doesn't understand how much she hurt me.

___ I lost something that can never be regained or repaid.

___ This person is not who I thought he was.

___ I would be too vulnerable without my anger.

___ Being a victim gets me sympathy from others.

___ I am afraid of the pain that lies beneath my anger.

___ I might have to claim some responsibility for the relationship breach.

___ I don't want to be hurt again.

__ I want revenge.

The fact is, you will forgive when you decide that your personal List B is costing you too much to maintain.

Take a moment to go through List A and check off the items that apply to you. Which items cause you the most pain? Now take another look at List B and measure each item against the price you pay in holding onto your bitterness and resentment. Check those items you are willing either to let go or to deal with in a more constructive way. Finally, bring your lists into God's presence and ask Him for the strength and wisdom you need to start making healthy changes in your response to relationship hurts.

Deciding to forgive not only releases you from the painful costs in List A but also opens you to resources that can make forgiving easier: love, patience, peace, self-control—in fact, all the fruit of a mature Christian spirit.[1]

Today's Fitness Challenge - Day 5

☑ FEED YOUR SOUL: *"Let all bitterness, and wrath, and anger, and clamor, and evil speaking, be put away from you, with all malice."*

—Ephesians 4:31 (KJV)

☑ LISTEN TO FORGIVENESS: I can stop paying the price of unforgiveness any time I want.

☑ CHECK YOUR HEART: Which pain in List A will be the most difficult for me to give up? Why?

☑ KEEP GOING: With God's help, I will realize when I am causing my own pain by refusing to forgive.

Bonus Challenge

1. What is my most painful memory? What happened, when did it happen, and who was responsible for hurting me? Is part of that original pain still with me?

2. How do I typically respond to pain in a relationship? Is there anything I do that is missing from List A?

3. Create a List C with the title, "I can forgive, even though..." Rewrite each statement in List B from this perspective of forgiving. For example, the first statement can be rewritten: "I can forgive, even though I may never get an apology."

Week Two
My Fitness Log

☑ *Complete each statement as found in the lesson indicated.* *

1.   More important than _____ is learning to _____
     _____. *(DAY 1)*

2.   _____ your enemies and _____ for those who
     persecute you. *(DAY 1)*

3.   Every _____ experience places you at a new
     _____. *(DAY 2)*

4.   In _____ we have a perfect model of how to
     _____ to _____ _____. *(DAY 2)*

5.   Draw _____ to God, and He will _____ _____ to
     you. *(DAY 3)*

6.   Your _____ is _____ the person who hurt you. *(DAY 3)*

7.   He who _____ his sins does not prosper, but
     whoever _____ and _____ them finds mercy.
     (DAY 4)

8.   Mercy is a _____, not a _____. *(DAY 4)*

9.   It is better to suffer for _____ _____, if suffering
     should be God's will, than to suffer for _____
     _____. *(DAY 5)*

10. _____ forgiveness is a common strategy for
     responding to relationship pain. *(DAY 5)*

* See Appendix A for answer key.

☑ Record the most important lesson you learned this week.

☑ Write a prayer to God. Tell Him truthfully what is in your
   heart at this stage of your walk and ask Him for what you
   need to continue.

Week Two
Weekend Workout

Forgiveness Prayer

THE WARM-UP. Read aloud Psalm 130:

Out of the depths I cry to you, O LORD;
*   O LORD, hear my voice.*
Let your ears be attentive
*   to my cry for mercy.*
If you, O LORD, kept a record of sins,
*   O LORD, who could stand?*
But with you there is forgiveness;
*   therefore you are feared.*
I wait for the LORD, my soul waits,
*   and in his word I put my hope.*
My soul waits for the LORD
*   more than watchmen wait for the morning,*
*   more than watchmen wait for the morning.*
O Israel, put your hope in the LORD,
*   for with the LORD is unfailing love*
*   and with him is full redemption.*
He himself will redeem Israel
*   from all their sins.*

THE STRETCH. Read the psalm again, but this time silently and prayerfully. Ask the Holy Spirit to pray through the psalm with you.

In what ways can you identify with the psalmist?

Which verse in particular captures your attention? Take a few moments now to meditate on that verse.

THE WORKOUT. In the Gospel of Luke we read, "One day Jesus was praying in a certain place. When he finished, one of His disciples said to Him, 'Lord, teach us to pray, just as John taught his disciples.'"[1]

Jesus' disciples already knew how to pray. As pious Jews, they had been raised on prayer and knew all the rules: how to dress, how to stand, what words to use, when and where they should pray. But they had also been observing Jesus. They had watched how He prayed, how often He prayed, how spontaneously He prayed. They knew better than anyone that He always prayed before He acted and that prayer made Him strong and focused and centered in the will of the Father. They wanted to learn His secret for such effective prayer.

Jesus responded to their request by teaching them what has come to be called the Lord's Prayer. It is a simple, adaptable model that contains all the elements we need to pray effectively.

Earnest prayer is an important spiritual discipline that will help you on your daily walk with forgiveness. Below is a table that adapts elements of the Lord's Prayer into a forgiveness prayer. Follow the table's recommendations to compose your own prayer in the space provided below the table.

Elements of the Lord's Prayer[2]	Adapt Elements Into a Forgiveness Prayer
Our Father in heaven,	Address your prayer as Jesus did, to the loving Father who cares for you.
hallowed be your name,	Honor God for who He is.
your kingdom come,	Express your desire to see God rule in your life and your relationships.
your will be done on earth as it is in heaven.	Surrender your words, actions, and attitudes to God's redemptive purpose.
Give us today our daily bread.	Ask God for what you need to love and to forgive. Be specific.
Forgive us our debts,	Confess how you have wronged others, and ask God to forgive you.
as we also have forgiven our debtors.	Name others' sins against you that you have not forgiven. Ask God to help you forgive each one.
And lead us not into temptation,	Renounce whatever keeps you locked in unforgiveness. Ask for help in resisting specific attitudes and behaviors.
but deliver us from the evil one.	Acknowledge Satan's efforts to lead you away from love and forgiveness. Ask God to rescue and protect you.

My Forgiveness Prayer

_____

_____

_____

_____

_____

_____

_____

_____

_____

_____

_____

_____

THE COOL-DOWN. Read through your forgiveness prayer, asking the Holy Spirit to pray it with you. Which lines seem especially meaningful? Mark them and take a few moments now to meditate on them.

Close the session by praying these simple words, known by many as the Jesus Prayer:

Lord Jesus Christ,
    Son of God,
have mercy on me, a sinner.

Lord Jesus Christ,
    Son of God,
have mercy on [*my debtor*], a sinner.
            — Amen.

Week Three

Though I walk in the midst of trouble,
you preserve my life;
you stretch out your hand against the anger of my foes,
with your right hand you save me. (Psalm 138:7)

Week Three
Day 1

Hidden Treasures

As Jesus was starting out on his way to Jerusalem, a man came running up to him, knelt down, and asked, "Good Teacher, what must I do to inherit eternal life?"

"Why do you call me good?" Jesus asked. "Only God is truly good. But to answer your question, you know the commandments: 'You must not murder. You must not commit adultery. You must not steal. You must not testify falsely. You must not cheat anyone. Honor your father and mother.'"

"Teacher," the man replied, "I've obeyed all these commandments since I was young."

Looking at the man, Jesus felt genuine love for him. "There is still one thing you haven't done," he told him. "Go and sell all your possessions and give the money to the poor, and you will have treasure in heaven. Then come, follow me."

At this the man's face fell, and he went away sad, for he had many possessions. (Mark 10:17–22, NLT)

If you are reluctant to forgive, you may have hidden a treasure for yourself somewhere in the wounding experience.

A treasure can be anything that a person greatly values and would sacrifice much to keep or to acquire. In the above story Jesus points out a conflict of treasures in the heart of a man who comes to Him for advice. The man has wealth and social status, yet he feels a hole in his life. He yearns for a place in God's kingdom. He has a clear sense of himself as a good and careful keeper of God's laws, and his wealth seems to be evidence of God's blessing. Nevertheless, he asks the Teacher, as one "good" man to another, how he can satisfy the unfulfilled longing of his soul.

Loving him and wanting to redeem him, Jesus lays before this man a choice: You may have treasure in heaven, He says, or treasure on earth, but not both. Elsewhere, Jesus warns that our loyalties and priorities in life will be determined by what we value most; that is, our hearts will be found close to whatever we treasure.[1] If we treasure our relationship with God above everything else, then our lives will reflect kingdom values: we will love God and express love for each other through acts of service, sacrifice, and peacemaking. Earthly treasure, by contrast, takes our eyes off God and displaces the authority and power of His love in our hearts. We are told that the man in the story went away sad because he valued his earthly possessions more than the prospect of God's kingdom. We may infer that he was not willing to give up the earthly benefits of wealth or his pride as a pious Jew for the intangible benefits of loving God and trusting in His promises of mercy and eternal life.

Scripture teaches that forgiveness is a kingdom value.[2] When we love and forgive each other, we secure benefits that we need to be spiritually fit for God's kingdom. An unforgiving attitude, on the other hand, may tempt us with earthly benefits, as the following chart describes:

Treasures Hidden in Unforgiveness	Earthly Benefits
Anger	My righteous anger makes me feel powerful and makes other people respect me.

Approval	My forgiving would disappoint and alienate people whose opinions matter to me.
Belonging	I enjoy commiserating with people who have been mistreated as I have been.
Blame	I can focus on my offender's bad behavior and ignore my own faults.
Comfort	I am settled in my role as the wounded party; much of my life is organized around what happened to me.
Free pass	My bad decisions and behaviors can be excused because of what I have suffered.
Identity	I like to describe myself in terms of my injury, such as the victim of an unfaithful spouse.
Pain	I have lived with my pain for so long, I could not give it up; my pain makes me feel real and keeps me focused.
Pride	I can boast that I am a better person than the one who hurt me.
Reputation	I enjoy being known as a person with spine who does not forgive easily and is always right.

Righteousness	I merit God's acceptance more than my offender does; I hold the higher moral ground.
Rights	I did not deserve to be treated poorly and am entitled to an apology and restitution.
Safety	My forgiving would invite my offender or others to hurt me again.
Satisfaction	I enjoy punishing my offender by withholding love and forgiveness.
Security	I know how to live as a victim, but I don't know how to live a larger life.
Strength	My forgiving would make me look weak and passive.
Testimony	I feel affirmed when I tell others the story of how I was wronged.

Like the rich man in the story, we must choose between the riches of earthly life or those of God's kingdom.

Today's Fitness Challenge - Day 1

☑ FEED YOUR SOUL: *"Command them to do good, to be rich in good deeds, and to be generous and willing to share. In this way they will lay up treasure for themselves as a firm foundation for the coming age, so that they may take hold of the life that is truly life."*
—1 Timothy 6:18-19

☑ LISTEN TO FORGIVENESS: My choices reveal the treasures I have hidden in my heart.

☑ CHECK YOUR HEART: Which earthly benefits do I treasure that have kept me from forgiving?

☑ KEEP GOING: With God's help, I will identify the earthly treasures hidden in my unwillingness to forgive and will let them go.

Bonus Challenge

1. What have I sacrificed in order to keep those treasures I have hidden in unforgiveness? In other words, what would become available to me as I give up my unforgiving attitude?

2. Recreate the "Treasures" chart with a new title, "Treasures Hidden in Forgiveness." Describe the benefits for each treasure as they reflect kingdom values. Cite Scripture support wherever possible.

3. If I knelt before Jesus as the rich man did and asked His advice, what is the one treasure He would command me to give up in order to follow Him? How would my life and my relationships change if I were willing to obey Him?

Week Three
Day 2

Hopeful Remorse

The LORD spoke to Manasseh and his people, but they paid no attention. So the LORD brought against them the army commanders of the king of Assyria, who took Manasseh prisoner, put a hook in his nose, bound him with bronze shackles and took him to Babylon. In his distress he sought the favor of the LORD his God and humbled himself greatly before the God of his fathers. And when he prayed to him, the LORD was moved by his entreaty and listened to his plea; so he brought him back to Jerusalem and to his kingdom. Then Manasseh knew that the LORD is God. (2 Chronicles 33:10-13)

When Judas, who had betrayed him, saw that Jesus was condemned, he was seized with remorse and returned the thirty silver coins to the chief priests and the elders. "I have sinned," he said, "for I have betrayed innocent blood."

"What is that to us?" they replied. "That's your responsibility."

So Judas threw the money into the temple and left. Then he went away and hanged himself. (Matthew 27:3-5)

Sorrow over our sins can either remake us or destroy us.

If only I could take it back... We have all spoken these helpless, painful words in moments of profound regret. After the heat of an argument has passed or the passion of a greedy or lustful obsession has subsided, we may suffer the agony of realizing that we acted wrongly or foolishly, perhaps hurtfully or even wickedly. We may learn new information that changes our understanding of a situation or an adversary. At such times we want to relive the moment just before our transgression and make a different choice. We want to undo the harm we have done.

Unfortunately, we can do nothing to change what is already in the past. When conscience stings us with remorse, we have only two choices: to look back with hopeless regret or to look forward with hopeful expectation.

The Old Testament story of King Manasseh's repentance illustrates the remaking of a wicked man's life because of hopeful remorse. Manasseh was the son of Hezekiah, who was a descendent of David and a godly king of eighth-century Judah. Hezekiah turned his people away from foreign gods and led them in worshipping the one true God. When Manasseh came to the throne, however, he cast aside the God of his fathers. King Manasseh despised the teachings of Hezekiah and the prophets of his time: "[Manasseh] did evil in the eyes of the LORD, following the detestable practices of the nations the LORD had driven out before the Israelites."[1]

Manasseh rebuilt the high places for worshipping idols, which his father had destroyed; he erected Asherah poles and altars to Baal and even built altars in the temple itself to worship false gods. He practiced astrology and witchcraft, sought out mediums and spiritists, and sacrificed his children to foreign gods. He killed the prophets and those who remained faithful to the Lord God of Israel. Worst of all, he ruled as king for thirteen years and "led Judah and the people of Jerusalem astray, so that they did more evil than the nations the LORD had destroyed before the Israelites."[2] Manasseh was one of the wickedest kings ever to rule over God's people.

Manasseh's day of reckoning came when the Assyrian army showed up, put a hook in his nose, and hauled him off to Babylon, which at that time was a province of Assyria. He spent twelve years in prison, plenty of time to reflect on his terrible crimes. He remembered the God of his father, Hezekiah, and at some point Manasseh came to grips with his guilt and his need for God's mercy. He "humbled himself greatly before the God of his fathers."

That must have been an amazing prayer because God, who alone can see into a person's heart, heard his plea and "was moved by his entreaty." God responded by getting Manasseh released from prison, bringing him back to Jerusalem, and restoring his kingdom to him. This turn of events was nothing short of miraculous! "Then Manasseh knew that the Lord is God." Another translation says, "Then Manasseh finally realized that the LORD alone is God!"[3] Manasseh humbled himself and repented of his truly terrible sins, and God responded with such an astonishing show of forgiveness and grace that Manasseh could no longer doubt the Lord's sovereignty.

We are perhaps more familiar with the New Testament story of Judas Iscariot, the friend and disciple of Jesus who sold out his master for thirty silver coins. Like Manasseh, Judas realized the wickedness of his actions and "was seized with remorse." Unlike Manasseh, however, Judas did not turn to God and humble himself but tried to undo the harm himself. He offered to return the money, and when the chief priests refused him, he threw the coins away. This act, even for a man who loved money as much as Judas did, nevertheless failed to relieve him of his guilt. Driven by hopeless remorse, seeing no way out of his torment, Judas "went away and hanged himself."

Hopeful remorse, like Manasseh's, has the power to transform a life because it turns us back to God. Such remorse is hopeful because it is rooted in faith that God has the power and the will to meet us in our weakness and sin, to heal our sorrow, and to give us what we need to change our attitudes and behaviors for the better. When we repent and make God the center of our attention, our hope is no longer rooted in our own resources but in the infinite wisdom, grace, and strength of our Father, who loves us and wants the best for us. God will even transform the memory of our sin—instead of a source of pain and shame, it becomes the occasion for rejoicing as we remember how God stepped in to save us and make us holy.

Remorse like Judas's, on the other hand, is hopeless because sin remains trapped in self-attention. We may feel guilty about our wrongdoing, yet in our pride we refuse to seek out God and admit our need for His help. Like Judas, we try to fix the problem ourselves. Hopeless remorse locks us in the past as we endlessly ruminate about how stupidly or selfishly or malevolently we behaved. Such brooding leads to bitterness and self-loathing—we suffer mentally and physically and may find ourselves on a slippery slope into deeper sin. Still our pride keeps us from seeking God; guilt and sorrow over our sin are worthless without the humility that leads us to healing and transformation of character.

Hopeful remorse was the remaking of King Manasseh's life. After he repented in the Assyrian prison, God gave him twenty more years to rule over Judah, and Manasseh made good use of his time. He got rid of the idols in the high places; he removed the Asherah poles and the altars to foreign gods. He restored the temple altar of the Lord and led the people in worshipping the one true God of Israel. Although he could not undo all the evil that he had done, his life nevertheless became an irrefutable testimony to the saving grace of the Lord his God.

In contrast, Judas's hopeless remorse led to his destruction. He refused to turn to God in humility and to repent of his crimes. His saved and transformed life might have been a powerful testimony as he went among strangers and proclaimed the gospel message of God's love and forgiveness as one who had experienced it firsthand. Instead, rather than submit to God he chose to kill himself along with the compelling witness that his surrendered life might have brought to the world.

Today's Fitness Challenge - Day 2

☑ FEED YOUR SOUL: *"Godly sorrow brings repentance that leads to salvation and leaves no regret, but worldly sorrow brings death."*

—2 Corinthians 7:10

☑ LISTEN TO FORGIVENESS: Hopeless remorse traps me in the past, but hopeful remorse opens me to a different future.

☑ CHECK YOUR HEART: Am I more familiar with hopeful remorse or hopeless remorse?

☑ KEEP GOING: With God's help, I will stop dwelling on past mistakes that I cannot change and give my future to Him.

Bonus Challenge

1. Which regrets from my past have I allowed to eat away at me? How have these regrets hurt my relationships with others? with myself? with God?

2. Why is loading myself with self-recriminations often more attractive to me than seeking God's forgiveness? Why do I cling to my guilt so tenaciously?

3. What do I think of the statement, "Guilt and sorrow over our sin are worthless without humility"?

Week Three
Day 3

Indifference Hurts

When I look at the night sky and see the work of your fingers –
   the moon and the stars you set in place –
what are mere mortals that you should think about them,
   human beings that you should care for them? (Psalm 8:3–4,
NLT)

Indifference hurts because it says, "I don't care about you."

As humans, we need to believe that we matter. We derive purpose and meaning for our lives by the work we do and by the relationships in which we invest ourselves. We like to think that our daily activities make a difference in the world, that we are significant, that we are *valued.*

Losing a job or being passed over for a promotion might crush us because such actions threaten us with the frightening possibility that we don't matter. Even more devastating can be the loss of an important personal relationship. We learn about ourselves from the ways in which others reflect us. We gauge our attractiveness, our likeability, our cleverness, our giftedness, our *value* from the responses of people around us, especially those who are closest to us. When people treat us indifferently, they stop reflecting us. Such indifference from a spouse, a child, a parent, or an intimate friend hurts and scares us because it shakes our confidence in who we believe ourselves to be.

In a caring relationship, the sudden indifference of one person toward the other is inevitably perceived by that other as abandonment. When we have been hurt or betrayed, we may withdraw from the relationship to "nurse our wounds"; it is normal to take some time to process the event mentally and emotionally and prepare ourselves to reengage. Unfortunately, we may also withdraw with the intent of punishing the other. We know we can hurt back by withholding what others need from us and giving them the "cold shoulder." In extreme cases, we may sever the relationship entirely and treat the other person as if he or she no longer exists and has been erased from memory.

Indifference can feel worse than verbal abuse or physical violence. A child may misbehave to get a parent's attention, preferring negative attention to no attention at all. Victims of domestic violence may tolerate physical and emotional torment as a kind of reassurance that they at least *matter* to their abusive partner.

God created us for relationship with each other, but most importantly for relationship with Himself. We suffer most when our lifeline with God feels severed, and we believe that God has abandoned us. Even secular psychologists recognize the spiritual crisis of a believer who feels that God has become indifferent. From the cross, Jesus Himself does not cry out in physical pain so much as in the anguish of feeling His Father's turning away, as He quotes from the psalmist: "My God, my God, why have you forsaken me?"[1] Facing the possibility that we no longer matter to God is a heartache too terrible to bear.

Because of the price Jesus paid on the cross for our sins, we never have to face that same anguish of God's turning away from us. Far from being indifferent, God's love for us is strong and steady.[2] When we sin and feel separated from God, what we perceive as God's withdrawing from us in displeasure is, in fact, our own withdrawing from God. Prompted by pride, shame, fear, or confusion, we are the ones who become indifferent. In our weakness and brokenness, we cut ourselves off from the very One who can make us strong and whole.

Likewise, in our human relationships we often cut ourselves off for the same reasons of pride, shame, fear, or confusion. Our indifference can be a cover to disguise the truth that the other person *does* matter, so much, in fact, that we take extreme measures to protect ourselves from further injury by erecting this false pretense. Under such circumstances, forgiveness and reconciliation with this person are impossible.

The remedy for a relationship standoff is to admit, first to yourself and then to the other person, how much that other person does matter to you. Even if he or she does not respond to you in the way you would wish, you can break through the wall of indifference that separates you and free yourself to love again. Your honesty and accessibility will demonstrate more than anything your genuine desire to heal and restore your relationship.

Today's Fitness Challenge - Day 3

☑ FEED YOUR SOUL: *"I know you well — you are neither hot nor cold; I wish you were one or the other! But since you are merely lukewarm, I will spit you out of my mouth!"*
— Revelation 3:15-16 (TLB)

☑ LISTEN TO FORGIVENESS: I cannot love or forgive through my wall of indifference.

☑ CHECK YOUR HEART: How has my indifference damaged a relationship?

☑ KEEP GOING: With God's help, I will find the courage to break through my wall of indifference and love others transparently.

Bonus Challenge

1. How do I feel when others treat me with indifference? How do I typically respond when someone withdraws from me? What do I hope to gain by such a response?

2. When I withdraw from a relationship, is the reason more to protect myself or to punish the other person? Is withdrawing ever beneficial? Is it ever right to rebuff the other person's attempts to reestablish a relationship with me?

3. Sometimes indifference can feel like forgiveness. How are they alike, and how are they different? Compare the roots and the fruits of each.

Week Three
Day 4

The Perfect Goal

You have heard that it was said, "Love your neighbor and hate your enemy." But I tell you: Love your enemies and pray for those who persecute you, that you may be sons of your Father in heaven. He causes his sun to rise on the evil and the good, and sends rain on the righteous and the unrighteous. If you love those who love you, what reward will you get? Are not even the tax collectors doing that? And if you greet only your brothers, what are you doing more than others? Do not even pagans do that? Be perfect, therefore, as your heavenly Father is perfect. (Matthew 5:43–48)

God alone is capable of perfect forgiveness.

Perfection in the spiritual sense implies a completeness or wholeness that is like God. Scripture describes God as perfect in His law, in His way and His word, in His works, and in His nature.[1] Everything that God is or says or does is wholly good, wholly moral, and wholly free from fault or blemish. His purpose and actions are always consistent with His character. Even His very presence is complete: He never withholds a part of Himself but makes Himself fully available to us in our relationship with Him.

Jesus is both our model and our means for human perfection in the Father.[2] The only human to ever live a life wholly obedient to the Father and completely devoid of sin, Jesus established a new covenant between the perfect Father and His people. Through Jesus' sacrifice on the cross, our sins are forgiven, and we are declared whole and righteous before God. Even though we continue to sin and fall short of Jesus' example, God covers us with His Son's righteousness and sees us as perfect.

In the Matthew passage quoted above, Jesus used the Greek word *teleios* in His exhortation that we should be perfect as the Father is perfect. By using "perfect" in its future tense, He indicated not that God expects sinless perfection from us in this world but that we should strive for a moral uprightness that imitates the Father's perfection. Motivated by our love for God, we cooperate with the Holy Spirit's transforming grace in our lives to bring us closer and closer to Christ's example of perfection. Indeed, our highest aspiration becomes a fullness and completeness that can only be achieved in God's eternal kingdom when we will be glorified and completed in Christ.[3]

To be perfect as the Father is perfect is to love as the Father loves. His love is perfect because He is perfect and His very nature is love.[4] His love is always available, always complete and unconditional. He never allows anger or bitterness to stand in the way of His relationship with us. His patience and generosity are inexhaustible. No matter how we deny Him, reject Him, silence Him, ridicule His ways, or forsake Him for other gods, He calls us back with a steadfast love that never fails.[5] His love for us does not depend upon the way we treat Him. He loves only because of who He is, because His very nature is pure and perfect love.

Moreover, God's forgiveness is perfect because it flows from His perfect love. His forgiveness is never partial, never conditional, never manipulative. Once given, it is never retracted and never has to be given again. It has no objective other than to heal a broken relationship and to recover the beloved who for a time was lost and wandering. Through His perfect forgiveness the Father brings us fully into His presence and lavishes on us unlimited love, mercy, tenderness, and joyful companionship. He gives us full rights of adoption into His family. He sends His precious Spirit to live in our innermost being so that we need never again feel lost or afraid or alone. He stands ready to supply our every need if we will allow Him.

By telling us to be perfect as the Father is perfect, Jesus commissioned us to bring holiness not only into our own lives but also into our communities. In loving one another, we cooperate with the Spirit's efforts to grow us spiritually and to advance God's kingdom in our midst. We show our love for God by showing love and justice to one another. Jesus pronounced the peacemakers to be blessed "for they will be called sons of God."[6] Promoting peace is a holy task. Christ's mission was to bring peace, reconciling people with one another and with God. When we minister in the world as peacemakers, we reflect the very character that identifies us with the Father and with the family of faith. We distinguish ourselves from those who care nothing about God or His laws of love.

Despite our best efforts, neither our love nor our forgiveness will be perfect this side of heaven. Nevertheless, the Father sustains us with His own perfect love and mercy, and the Spirit works miracles in our imperfections. Through Christ we can be confident that we have been made perfect even as the Spirit continues to make us holy.[7]

Today's Fitness Challenge - Day 4

☑ FEED YOUR SOUL: *"Be imitators of God, therefore, as dearly loved children and live a life of love, just as Christ loved us and gave himself up for us as a fragrant offering and sacrifice to God."*
— Ephesians 5:1-2

☑ LISTEN TO FORGIVENESS: Christ calls me to be a minister of God's perfect peace in this world.

☑ CHECK YOUR HEART: How has my forgiving been less than perfect or complete?

☑ KEEP GOING: With God's help, I will yield my relationship hurts to the perfecting influence and nurture of the Holy Spirit.

Bonus Challenge

1. What usually motivates me to forgive? What usually keeps me from forgiving?

2. Have I accepted God's perfect and complete offering of forgiveness, or are there areas of my life for which I do not feel forgiven? What would it take for me to fully accept God's offer? How would my complete acceptance of God's forgiveness help me to forgive others?

3. Sometimes, especially when I have been wounded deeply, I find myself revisiting my anger and resentment even after I have forgiven my offender. Does this mean my forgiveness was insincere? Why does forgiveness often feel like a multi-step process?

Week Three
Day 5

Called to God's Business

Since you have been chosen by God who has given you this new kind of life, and because of his deep love and concern for you, you should practice tenderhearted mercy and kindness to others. Don't worry about making a good impression on them but be ready to suffer quietly and patiently. Be gentle and ready to forgive; never hold grudges. Remember, the Lord forgave you, so you must forgive others. (Colossians 3:12–13, TLB)

As a Christian, you have been hired into God's business to do a job.

Signing on with God means buying into His corporate agenda. And that agenda is the salvation of the world. His company philosophy is straightforward: As mercy has been shown to you, go and do likewise.[1]

God takes you on not because of your polished résumé or because He needs you to help Him with His mission but simply because He loves you. His general notice for hire invites *anyone* to apply for the job, regardless of personal beauty, intellectual prowess, or track record of good works. In fact, He often chooses those whom the world deems as poor or having little to offer, and rewards them with corporate dividends of faith and eternal stock in His company.[2] His one requirement for hire is a humble and contrite heart, an asset He cannot supply but that you must have in order to meet the tasks He assigns you.[3]

When you wear the badge that identifies you as belonging

to God, then He puts all His company resources at your disposal. He provides an Operations Manual to instruct you. He assigns you a Personal Tutor, who is always as near as a prayer. He gives you a direct line so you can always reach Him and speak to Him personally. He promises to meet with you anytime you say and to sit with you for as long as you want. He supplies mentors within the company who can show you by example how certain tasks can be accomplished and to sponsor you when you need accountability. He provides a history of stories that demonstrate the nature and depth of His love. Best of all, He guarantees that your contract with Him will never be revoked or revised, that the privileges of belonging to Him are impartial and eternal, and that your protection under His Name is absolute and inviolable.

And what does this Corporate Head require of you? He expects you to act justly, to value mercy, and to live a humble life submitted to His leadership.[4] In other words, He expects you to live out the company philosophy of loving and forgiving others in exactly the same manner as He has loved and forgiven you. You are to study His example and to conduct yourself as an ambassador of His company, reflecting the heart and character of its Leader by your words and actions. If you do your job as God intends, then others will come to associate your company badge with expectations of being treated fairly and respectfully. They will wonder at a policy that values forgiveness over retaliation and pursues the healing of relationships and hearts over the collecting of outstanding debts. They will be curious about benefits that are free to anyone who applies because the CEO's Son has already paid the fee for all.

And how does this CEO evaluate your performance on the job? He measures your success not by the brilliance of your achievements but by the faithfulness of your obedience. Worldly standards of success do not apply, for it is impossible to fail with

Him, just as it is impossible to succeed without Him. In confessing the very weaknesses that the world despises, you learn to be strong and wise in God. In dismantling the pride that protects and promotes you in the world, you are released to discover how your unloving attitudes may hurt and discourage the people around you. In understanding how desperately you need God's mercy, you become a competent minister of mercy to others. Thus, through your obedience and careful attention to God's on-the-job training, you will find yourself equipped for every task He assigns to you as you respond in faith to His calling.[5]

Today's Fitness Challenge - Day 5

☑ FEED YOUR SOUL: *"For we are God's workmanship, created in Christ Jesus to do good works, which God prepared in advance for us to do."*

—Ephesians 2:10

☑ LISTEN TO FORGIVENESS: Forgiveness is a job skill that I can learn and practice.

☑ CHECK YOUR HEART: What qualifies me to do God's work of forgiving others?

☑ KEEP GOING: With God's help, I will meet the challenges of the job He has hired me to do.

Bonus Challenge

1. How many different company badges do I wear in a week? Which badge am I most likely to show to others? least likely?

2. How can I become more skilled at forgiving others? What aspects of forgiveness are still the most difficult for me to understand and practice? Where can I get the instruction I need?

3. Who in God's company has mentored me and shown me what it means to work for God? To whom could I turn for help in learning how "to act justly, value mercy, and live a humble life submitted to [God's] leadership"?

Week Three
My Fitness Log

☑ *Complete each statement as found in the lesson indicated.* *

1. We must choose between the riches of _____ _____ or those of _____ _____. *(DAY 1)*

2. My _____ reveal the _____ I have hidden in my heart. *(DAY 1)*

3. Sorrow over our sins can either _____ us or _____ us. *(DAY 2)*

4. _____ remorse traps me in the past, but _____ remorse opens me to a different future. *(DAY 2)*

5. As humans, we need to believe _____ _____ _____. *(DAY 3)*

6. When people treat us _____, they stop _____ us. *(DAY 3)*

7. God alone is capable of _____ _____. *(DAY 4)*

8. Jesus is both our _____ and our _____ for human perfection in the Father. *(DAY 4)*

9. As mercy has been shown to you, go and _____ _____. *(DAY 5)*

10. Forgiveness is a _____ _____ that I can _____ and _____. *(DAY 5)*

* See Appendix A for answer key.

☑ Record the most important lesson you learned this week.

☑ Write a prayer to God. Tell Him truthfully what is in your heart at this stage of your walk and ask Him for what you need to continue.

Week Three
Weekend Workout

Truth or Myth?

THE WARM-UP. Read aloud from Proverbs 2:

My son, if you accept my words
    and store up my commands within you,
turning your ear to wisdom
    and applying your heart to understanding,
and if you call out for insight
    and cry aloud for understanding,
and if you look for it as for silver
    and search for it as for hidden treasure,
then you will understand the fear of the LORD
    and find the knowledge of God.
For the LORD *gives wisdom,*
    and from his mouth come knowledge and understanding.
He holds victory in store for the upright,
    he is a shield to those whose walk is blameless,
for he guards the course of the just
    and protects the way of his faithful ones.
Then you will understand what is right and just
    and fair – every good path.
For wisdom will enter your heart,
    and knowledge will be pleasant to your soul.
Discretion will protect you,
    and understanding will guard you.
Wisdom will save you from the ways of wicked men,
    from men whose words are perverse,

who leave the straight paths
  to walk in dark ways,
who delight in doing wrong
  and rejoice in the perverseness of evil,
whose paths are crooked
  and who are devious in their ways.
                    – Proverbs 2:1–15

THE STRETCH. Read the passage again, but this time silently and prayerfully. Ask the Holy Spirit to pray through the reading with you.

Underline or list separately all the benefits that God promises to those who diligently seek wisdom.

What in that list of benefits do you particularly need right now? Write it down, and take a few moments to talk with God about your need.

THE WORKOUT. The book of Proverbs has much to say about wisdom and the fear of the Lord. These two concepts come together in Proverbs 9: "Fear of the LORD is the foundation of wisdom. Knowledge of the Holy One results in good judgment."[1] The expression, *fear of the Lord*, means a reverent trust in God as the Creator and Sovereign Lord of all things. It means living our lives in acknowledgment of God's majesty and power, mindful that He is loving and merciful but also the righteous Judge and enemy of all that is evil. Making God the center of our understanding and acknowledging Him as the source of all knowledge and truth, Proverbs says, assures us of good judgment.

Like everything else about God, His knowledge is pure and complete, and it can be called *truth*. Human knowledge, on the other hand, is only a perception of truth. Our knowledge is limited by our finiteness and distorted by time, culture, and sin.[2] *Wisdom* corrects our distortions and aligns our perceptions and decisions with God's truth. We gain wisdom through our experience and the experience of others through shared history, through instruction, and from God Himself through His Word and divine revelation. The apostle Paul calls wisdom that is not centered in the fear of the Lord foolishness because it does not bring us closer to God's truth or help us to make choices that will please Him.[3] God Himself is our only source of true wisdom.

Although God established relationships, our perceptions about love and forgiveness and what we have a right to expect from each other come primarily through our culture. We learn the rules of engagement—or disengagement—from our parents, our teachers, our peers, our magazines. From infancy we are raised on cultural myths that are daily reinforced, and we take them into our hearts and believe them to be right and just because they are so deeply imbedded within us that they *must* be true.

You can test your own perceptions about forgiveness by taking the following quiz, which will expose the myths you've come to believe. Answers can be found in Appendix B.

Truth or Myth?

Decide whether each statement about forgiveness is truth (T) or myth (M). Appendix B offers an answer and rationale for each.

T M 1. My forgiveness is not complete until the other person accepts it.

T M 2. Forgotten offenses have the power to hurt us in the present.

T M 3. Forgiveness is the first step in healing from an intimate wound.

T M 4. When I forgive, I am saying that the offense no longer matters.

T M 5. Some offenses are so hurtful that nothing good can come from them.

T M 6. Everyone deserves a chance to be forgiven, no matter what the offense.

T M 7. Holding onto my anger and bitterness protects me from further hurt.

T M 8. The other person should understand my hurt without my having to explain it.

T M 9. Forgiving does not necessarily mean trusting the other person again.

T M 10. Although I may not get one, I deserve an apology from the person who offended me.

T M 11. Reconciliation is not possible until both parties acknowledge their own guilt.

T M 12. I cannot approach God in prayer if I am still angry with my offender.

T M 13. Forgiving a loved one is easier than forgiving a stranger.

T M 14. Some offenses are unforgivable.

T M 15. If I forgive an unrepentant offender, then I am shirking my moral responsibility to bring him or her to justice.

T M 16. The bigger the offense, the harder it is to forgive.

T M 17. Forgiving gives permission for the other person to continue the offensive behavior.

T M 18. Until the other person understands my perspective, I cannot fully heal from the offense.

T M 19. Memories of minor offenses may change over time, but memories of deep wounds remain intact.

T M 20. The goal of forgiveness is always reconciliation.

T M 21. Withholding forgiveness gives me power in the relationship.

T M 22. In forgiving, I give up the hope that the other person will repent.

T M 23. Forgiving someone conditionally is better than not forgiving at all.

T M 24. Forgiving makes me vulnerable to the other person.

T M 25. Forgiveness is self-sacrificing.

T M 26. If I wait long enough, a damaged relationship will usually heal itself.

T M 27. Forgiving another person tears down the personal boundaries between us.

T   M   28.   Only through forgiveness can a damaged relationship return to the way it was before the rift.

T   M   29.   Wanting to promote my own well-being is a legitimate reason to forgive.

T   M   30.   When two people fight, it is usually clear which person is the victim and which is the offender who needs forgiving.

THE COOL-DOWN. Compare your answers to the quiz with those in Appendix B. Note any discrepancies and consider the explanation for each answer. How do you feel about having your opinions challenged? Ask God to open your mind to the possibility that a deep-seated belief of yours may not be His truth.

Close the session by praying through these words from Job:

"So where does wisdom come from,
*   and where does understanding live?*
It is hidden from the eyes of every living thing,
*   even from the birds of the air.*
The places of destruction and death say,
*   'We have heard reports about it.'*
Only God understands the way to wisdom,
*   and he alone knows where it lives,*
because he looks to the farthest parts of the earth
*   and sees everything under the sky.*
When God gave power to the wind
*   and measured the water,*
when he made rules for the rain
*   and set a path for a thunderstorm to follow,*
then he looked at wisdom and decided its worth;

he set wisdom up and tested it.
Then he said to humans,
    'The fear of the LORD is wisdom;
    to stay away from evil is understanding.'"
                    — Job 28:20–28 (NCV)

Week Four

If you do whatever I command you and walk in my ways and do what is right in my eyes by keeping my statutes and commands, as David my servant did, I will be with you. (1 Kings 11:38)

Week Four
Day 1

Can I Forgive Myself?

See, O LORD, how distressed I am;
> *my stomach churns,*
my heart is wrung within me,
> *because I have been very rebellious. (Lamentations 1:20,*
NRSV)

It's not your job to forgive yourself but God's.

Popular today is the notion that we must seek forgiveness from ourselves as well as from others when we have done harm. Psychologists urge us to accept ourselves as we are and not to let our guilt and remorse rob us of self-esteem. Christian moralists remind us that we are made in God's image and therefore have innate worth and dignity. Our culture of moral relativism teaches us that feeling good about ourselves is more important than doing what's right. Well-meaning Christians, pastors included, downplay Scriptures that emphasize the seriousness of sin and instead urge us to be gentle with ourselves when we fall victim to our natural human weaknesses.

A healthy love of self is important, but as we emphasize self-tolerance, we become more confused about what to do with our guilt over sin. Sometimes we shrug off our guilt too readily and go about our lives with our hearts and habits unchanged. The significance of our sin seems not to register at a deep level. Pride and self-sufficiency override the voice of conscience that might prompt us to repent and experience real growth. At such times the phrase, "I have forgiven myself," essentially means, "There was nothing really wrong with me in the first place. My sins are not so bad as to warrant serious attention."

At the other extreme are times when remorse lies so heavily within us that we refuse to give up our guilty suffering. We brand ourselves with our sin and submit our lives, and sometimes our relationships, to the tyranny of self-torment. When we feel trapped by our guilt, we may use the phrase, "I cannot forgive myself," to mask a deeper meaning:

I do not deserve to be happy.

I, not God, am the ultimate judge and authority in my life.

I am special; I should be able to rise above the sins that cause others to stumble.

I am afraid to test God's promise to make a new creature of me.

I am not worth saving.

My pride will not allow me to accept myself as flawed and unable to meet my own standards of perfection.

I am not convinced that God wants to heal and restore me.

I understand, better than God, how much I should pay for my sins.

I should be able to achieve righteousness on my own.

I don't really believe that God loves me enough to completely forgive me.

To forgive ourselves may sometimes seem an attractive notion, yet in fact it has no biblical basis. Self-forgiveness enthusiasts may support their position with references to Jesus' teachings on love and forgiveness. From His famous command to "Love your neighbor as yourself,"[1] some will infer that we are also to forgive our neighbors as we forgive ourselves. Such inference is unfounded—although forgiveness may spring from love, it is not the same as love. Love is the condition that makes forgiveness possible. Others direct us to the Lord's Prayer, in which Jesus instructs us to forgive our debtors in the same way that God has forgiven us our own debts.[2] Although it is true that we are to seek God's forgiveness as well as to forgive others, Jesus makes no mention of forgiving *ourselves*.

In fact, nowhere in the Bible does God ever tell us that we must or even *should* forgive ourselves. Instead, He consistently reserves that authority for Himself. If we truly could forgive our own sins, then we would have no need for a Savior; punishment and redemption would somehow lie in our own hands. The truth is, the only way out from under the burden of our guilt and remorse is to give the burden over to God — to confess our wrongdoing, to humble ourselves and ask for *His* forgiveness, and then to accept the power of His mercy to heal and restore us.

This is not to say that God absolves us of the responsibility to make changes in our lives. The Gospel of John tells the story of an adulterous woman who is brought before Jesus for public condemnation. Jesus unexpectedly turns the tables on her accusers, and when none are left to condemn her, He says to her, "Neither do I condemn you; go your way; from now on sin no more."[3] Notice that Jesus does *not* say, "Forgive yourself, and sin no more." Instead, He reassures her that *He* has forgiven her, and then He directs her to change her ways.

Although we cannot forgive ourselves, neither does God leave us to drown in our sins. If we will allow the Spirit to convict us, and if we will humble ourselves and ask for God's mercy, then by His grace and strength we can transcend those sins and, as the Spirit directs us, change our ways for the better.

Today's Fitness Challenge - Day 1

☑ FEED YOUR SOUL: *"For God did not send his Son into the world to condemn the world, but to save the world through him."*
—John 3:17

☑ LISTEN TO FORGIVENESS: I cannot forgive my own sins, but God can.

☑ CHECK YOUR HEART: Are there sins in my life from which I have refused to let God release me?

☑ KEEP GOING: With God's help, I will surrender my shame and guilt to His cleansing mercy.

Bonus Challenge

1. In which instances have I released my guilt too quickly? How might things have been different if I had allowed myself to grasp the seriousness of my wrongdoing and asked God to help me change?

2. When have I preferred to hold onto my guilt and postponed the promise of God's healing mercy? Which of the reasons cited in the text could account for my refusal to let go of my guilt?

3. How do I show others that I have forgiven them? What do I require of others before I can believe that they have truly forgiven me? What further proof do I need from God before I will believe that He has washed away my wickedest sin?

Week Four
Day 2

A Little Yeast

Your boasting is not good. Don't you know that a little yeast works through the whole batch of dough? Get rid of the old yeast that you may be a new batch without yeast – as you really are. For Christ, our Passover lamb, has been sacrificed. Therefore let us keep the Festival, not with the old yeast, the yeast of malice and wickedness, but with bread without yeast, the bread of sincerity and truth. (1 Corinthians 5:6-8)

Accepting God's forgiveness but refusing to forgive others is like drinking from a life-giving well but refusing to swallow.

God values forgiveness because He values relationships. As proof of His love for us, He devised a plan of redemption, at great cost to Himself, to cover our sins with His Son's righteousness. When we accept God's forgiveness, He expects us to love and forgive others with the very same love He gives to us. Claiming the promise of God's mercy without letting it change our hearts toward others the Bible calls *hypocrisy*.

Jesus repeatedly condemned the Pharisees and other religious leaders for their hypocrisy, in the sense that they were play-actors who were preoccupied with an external show of devotion to God but not interested in changing internally. He called these men blind guides and whitewashed tombs, beautiful on the outside but on the inside full of death and corruption.[1] He further warned His disciples to be on guard against the "yeast" of these hypocritical religious leaders.[2]

Yeast That Spoils

Yeast was often used figuratively in the Bible to indicate a corruptive influence. In the Jewish household, yeast was used in small amounts to ferment, or "spoil," bread dough; as such, it was a source of uncleanness and was unfit for use in burnt offerings to God. Observance of Passover began with a ceremonial cleansing of the house to remove every speck of yeast, symbolizing the casting out of sin. In the New Testament, yeast was a symbol not only of sin itself but also of the diffusive nature of sin—a little bit of sin has a corrupting influence that leads to further wickedness. Jesus decried the teachings of the Pharisees as corruptive because they were hypocritical: "What sorrow awaits you teachers of religious law and you Pharisees. Hypocrites! For you shut the door of the Kingdom of Heaven in people's faces. You won't go in yourselves, and you don't let others enter either."[3] Piety that is only for show leads us deeper into sin and further away from God.

Inevitably, the sin that cripples us internally will show up in our relationships. In the 1 Corinthians passage above, the apostle Paul used the image of yeast to symbolize the corrupting influence that our individual sins can bring into the body of believers. He warned that such influence must be removed before the entire community is damaged. We recognize the "yeast that spoils" in some familiar habits and attitudes that can trigger quarrels and escalate conflicts among us:

Yeast That Spoils	Habits and Attitudes that Spoil Relationships
Hypocrisy	My pretense of being perfect, morally superior, always right, justified in my opinions, or possessing

	all knowledge; believing myself to be specially favored by God and/or the world; professing innocence when I know I am guilty; accusing others of faults I carry within myself; expecting others to live up to my standards.
Deceit	My unwillingness to admit truth about the injury; blindness to faults or virtues of either myself or my offender; slanting the retelling of my story to make myself look good and my offender look bad; keeping secrets or perpetuating myths about myself or others; burying my anger, hurt, or sorrow with excessive busyness or forgetfulness; lying to avoid discomfort or discovery; attacking my offender indirectly because I fear honest confrontation.
Pride	My inflated sense of my own worth; the devaluing of my offender; my inability to tolerate criticism, the possibility that I am wrong, or the idea that I have sins to confess; being puffed up with good deeds or my own opinions; my inability to seek or to accept forgiveness from others; rigidity or stubbornness in my attitudes, beliefs, and behaviors toward my offender; my belief that I am entitled to extra considerations because I am somehow special.
Bitterness	My refusal to let go of anger; constantly dwelling on my pain and outrage; refusing to pray for my offender; hoping for the ruination of my offender; maligning my offender's reputation by gossiping and promoting ill-will; identifying myself primarily as a victim; planning my revenge, even if I don't carry it out; speaking words to my offender that are

	rude, critical, and debilitating.
Envy and Greed	My obsession with acquiring wealth, possessions, achievements, accolades, popularity, power, status, or whatever else gives me value in the eyes of the world; wishing ill on others because they have what I desire; lusting of the heart or the flesh that leads to quarrels and other sins; refusing to give up ground by admitting fault or forgiving my offender; resenting another's success.

The above list is far from complete but shows how even slightly negative attitudes and behaviors can gain a foothold until relationships are so damaged that forgiveness seems impossible.

Yeast That Builds Up

Perhaps surprisingly, Jesus also spoke figuratively of yeast as a *positive* spiritual influence: "The Kingdom of Heaven can be compared to a woman making bread. She takes a measure of flour and mixes in the yeast until it permeates every part of the dough."[4] The yeast is small and inconspicuous when first added to the dough, but its nature is to spread and grow and transform the flour mixture into fragrant, nourishing bread. Likewise, when we drink from the life-giving well and *swallow*, God's Spirit permeates our entire being, transforming us into agents for His kingdom. Even our smallest acts of obedience to the Spirit's leading permeate and transform the world around us.

Sincerity, the opposite of hypocrisy, is used six times in the New Testament to characterize a believer's life controlled by the Spirit.[5] We recognize the "yeast that builds up" as the qualities that grow and nourish our relationships and help us to forgive one another:

Yeast That Builds Up	Habits and Attitudes that Build Up Relationships
sincere love hatred of evil clinging to good brotherly devotion honoring of others joyful hope patience in affliction faithful prayer generosity hospitality harmonious relationships purity understanding patience kindness evidence of the Holy Spirit faithful preaching of truth clear conscience genuine faith wisdom from heaven love of peace consideration submission mercy good fruit	"Love must be sincere. Hate what is evil; cling to what is good. Be devoted to one another in brotherly love. Honor one another above yourselves....Be joyful in hope, patient in affliction, faithful in prayer. Share with God's people who are in need. Practice hospitality....Live in harmony with one another."[6] "We prove ourselves by our purity, our understanding, our patience, our kindness, by the Holy Spirit within us, and by our sincere love. We faithfully preach the truth."[7] "The purpose of my instruction is that all believers would be filled with love that comes from a pure heart, a clear conscience, and genuine faith."[8] "But the wisdom that comes from heaven is first of all pure; then peace-loving, considerate, submissive, full of mercy and good fruit, impartial and sincere. Peacemakers who sow in peace raise a harvest of righteousness."[9]

impartiality sincerity righteousness	

Your readiness to forgive depends upon the condition of your inner self. Decide which beliefs and attitudes you will allow to permeate your heart and your relationships. Choose whether you will be an agent in this world for the yeast that corrupts or the yeast that builds up community.

Today's Fitness Challenge - Day 2

☑ FEED YOUR SOUL: *"How seldom we weigh our neighbors in the same balance as ourselves."*
　　　　　　　　　　— Thomas à Kempis, 15th century monk

☑ LISTEN TO FORGIVENESS: The more honest I am with myself, the less fault I find in my neighbor.

☑ CHECK YOUR HEART: How has "yeast that spoils" gotten out of control in my life?

☑ KEEP GOING: With God's help, I will find the yeast that is spoiling my relationships and get rid of it before it does more harm.

Bonus Challenge

1. What images come to mind when I think of the word "corruption"? In what ways can relationships be corrupted?

2. List some characteristics of hypocrisy and contrast them with those of sincerity. Why was Jesus so condemning of hypocrisy among Jewish religious leaders?

3. Review the Habits & Attitudes under "Yeast That Spoils." Which corrupting influences have been most apparent in my relationships? How would my relationships change if I could get rid of this "old yeast"?

Week Four
Day 3

When Ends Justify Means

But Joseph told them, "Don't be afraid of me. Am I God, to judge and punish you? As far as I am concerned, God turned into good what you meant for evil, for he brought me to this high position I have today so that I could save the lives of many people. No, don't be afraid. Indeed, I myself will take care of you and your families." And he spoke very kindly to them, reassuring them. (Genesis 50:19–21, TLB)

Decide whether you would rather be right or be reconciled.

When someone offends you, forgiving your offender is probably not your first inclination. More likely, you will indulge in a sense of indignation and defend your right to feel offended. Even after some time has passed, and you've had a chance to cool off and think things over, you still may be unwilling to give up your perceived victimhood. Painful as the estrangement may be, difficult though the conflict may make your daily life, you nevertheless hold out for justice, even if a just outcome seems remote. You tell yourself, and anyone else who will listen, that others should pay for what you have suffered.

In the aftermath of being wounded, instant forgiveness is not always possible or even advisable. If the offense is serious, if a trust has been betrayed, then reconciling with the wounder cannot take place until you understand the significance of what you have lost and have begun to heal from the experience. The process of forgiving will take time; in the case of deep wounding, it may unfold over a lifetime.

Most conflicts, however, soon present the opportunity to reevaluate the situation and decide which goal is more important: holding out for justice or working to restore peaceful relations with the offending person.

If you value justice above reconciliation, then you will take an adversarial stance: you will use your words and actions to prove yourself right and to justify your wounded response. You may confront your offender openly and aggressively, or you may withdraw into a cold silence that nevertheless shouts your displeasure. You may gossip to harm the other's reputation and win emotional support for your position. Shaming, ridiculing, and undermining the other's efforts at work, at school, at church, or at home are also common means of retaliation. Even when you use calm reason and persuasion to insist upon your viewpoint, your stance is adversarial because your goal is to prove yourself right. You see yourself in a contest that you can win only by proving the other person to be wrong.

If, on the other hand, you believe that being right is less important than restoring a relationship, then you will take a conciliatory stance: you will use your words and actions to minister to the other person, to protect the relationship from further damage, and to honor the other person's reputation and well-being by refusing to gossip. You will show respect for the other person's viewpoint even if you don't agree with it. This conciliatory stance is forgiveness in action. By word and deed you affirm your esteem for the other person and your desire to remove the harmful barriers that stand between you.

The story of Joseph provides a poignant example of choosing reconciliation over justice.[1] If anyone had a right to bear a grudge and seek revenge, it was Joseph. His father's favorite, Joseph suffered the jealous retaliation of his brothers when they sold him into slavery at the age of seventeen and staged his bloody death. In Egypt, Joseph spent the next eleven years as a slave and two years in prison before his fortunes changed, and he was appointed governor. When severe famine brought his brothers literally to his doorstep to buy food, Joseph had the perfect opportunity to take his revenge on them. He had the power to order their executions or to sell them into slavery with as little mercy as they had shown him. Joseph did neither. Amazingly, he took pains to reassure them that they had nothing to fear from him and, further, that he would care for them and their families. "And he spoke very kindly to them." *Kindly.*

Joseph chose healing words and actions because his goal was to restore the relationship rather than to prove to his brothers that they had been wrong and cruel. When he could easily have justified his hatred for them, he reached out instead with love and forgiveness.

How fortunate we are to have a heavenly Father who also values reconciliation above justice! Although we deserve worse, He treats us in the same manner as Joseph—with kindness and patience. When He might condemn and punish us, He instead forgives us, not wanting to prolong our guilty suffering but rather to heal and restore us to Himself.

Today's Fitness Challenge - Day 3

☑ FEED YOUR SOUL: *"Do not seek revenge or bear a grudge against one of your people, but love your neighbor as yourself."*
— Leviticus 19:18

☑ LISTEN TO FORGIVENESS: In a relationship, insisting on being right often means being left.

☑ CHECK YOUR HEART: Has my stubborn need to be right ever damaged a relationship?

☑ KEEP GOING: With God's help, I will learn to value people more than I value my reputation for being right.

Bonus Challenge

1. Why is being right so important to me? In the home where I grew up, what happened when family members disagreed with each other? How were differences resolved?

2. Is it possible to have a relationship with someone who will not admit to being wrong? Why or why not?

3. Is it ever right to value justice over reconciliation and to take an adversarial stance? Can I actively oppose another's actions and still forgive him or her?

Week Four
Day 4

Surrender to Love

Therefore, as God's chosen people, holy and dearly loved, clothe yourselves with compassion, kindness, humility, gentleness and patience. Bear with each other and forgive whatever grievances you may have against one another. Forgive as the Lord forgave you. And over all these virtues put on love, which binds them all together in perfect unity.

Let the peace of Christ rule in your hearts, since as members of one body you were called to peace. And be thankful. Let the word of Christ dwell in you richly as you teach and admonish one another with all wisdom, and as you sing psalms, hymns and spiritual songs with gratitude in your hearts to God. And whatever you do, whether in word or deed, do it all in the name of the Lord Jesus, giving thanks to God the Father through him. (Colossians 3:12–17)

To forgive is to surrender your injury to love.

Surrendering means giving up your power and submitting yourself to the authority of another. Surrender is not passive but requires you to actively hand over the reigns to the conquering force. It means giving up your right to act on your own volition. It is acknowledging that a new agenda will determine your actions from now on.

Surrendering your injury to love is deciding to handle your relationship God's way. It means giving up your resentful feelings, your desire to damage the other person's reputation, or to take pleasure in the other person's suffering. It means giving up your right to seek revenge or to demand compensation for what you have suffered.

The Colossians passage quoted above describes how to handle a damaged relationship God's way. When you forgive in love the person who caused you harm, you are promising to treat this person with compassion and kindness, no matter how he or she treats you. You will act in ways that show you do not consider yourself to be better or holier or less sinful than this person. You are promising to treat this person with gentle care and patience.

Instead of stewing in resentment over what this person has taken from you, you will be free to notice the good things in your life. In the peace that comes from loving God, you will find the generosity to let your resentment go. Because recapturing this person's heart for the kingdom is important to God, it is important to you, too. You want God to use you however He will to bring grace and truth into the life of this person who hurt you.

Few of us enjoy the idea of surrendering ourselves to another power, yet we all do it. After we experience the surprise and pain of another's wrongful action against us, we face the decision of how we will respond; this point of decision is the moment of our surrender. We can choose to submit ourselves either to love or to love's antithesis, *self-promotion*. In our pain, in our confusion and anger and sorrow, our refusing to forgive may seem like the best course for protecting ourselves and our interests. It feels natural, and it is indeed the natural way of the world. In refusing to forgive, we are surrendering our injury to the world's principle of fortifying personal barriers to preserve and protect ourselves. This principle, however, runs contrary to God's kingdom principle, which recommends reaching across the barriers in love to heal and restore the other person as well as the relationship.

In refusing to forgive, we rewrite the Colossians passage in the interest of self-promotion:

Therefore, valuing my own interests over the desires of God's heart, I will clothe myself with selfish indifference, a critical eye to the faults of others, an air of superiority where it is warranted, harsh treatment when necessary to get my way, and impatience with those who do not live up to my expectations. Reluctant to admit my need for God's saving grace in my life, I will live by the principle of paying back evil in kind for the evil that is done to me.

I do not expect to live in peace or contentment. If I relax my guard, someone is sure to take advantage of me, so I will remain vigilant and keep others at a safe distance. Words such as love, joy, and gratitude have little meaning for me. I value power and prestige; I cannot get ahead in this world if people do not fear me. To give up my right to payback when someone has harmed me seems pointless and self-defeating. Forgiveness, for me, is not a reasonable option.

If we are honest, we must admit ownership to at least some of these sentiments. Each of us is familiar with surrendering to the authority of self-promotion. When we are angry or despairing over an injustice, it seems unfair of God to ask us to reach out in love and forgive the horrible person who hurt us. And it's true: it is unfair. It does not feel natural. We are neither motivated nor equipped to put our own interests aside and follow God's lead to love and forgive. Besides which, we have already surrendered the injury to love's antithesis. We've made our choice.

One of the great things about serving an almighty God is that nothing is impossible with Him! He stands ready and willing to redeem our voucher that says we've already chosen the other side. If we ask, He will supply us with not only the love and grace we need but also the motivation to extend these good gifts to the person who hurt us. He will use our love for Him to soften our hearts. Then He can use our forgiveness of others to soften their hearts as well.

Today's Fitness Challenge - Day 4

☑ FEED YOUR SOUL: *"Submit to God, and you will have peace."*

—Job 22:21 (NLT)

☑ LISTEN TO FORGIVENESS: Surrendering to love gets easier with practice.

☑ CHECK YOUR HEART: When has someone's unexpected act of generosity toward me softened my heart?

☑ KEEP GOING: With God's help, I will surrender everything about my injury to love — my thoughts, attitudes, memories, desires, feelings, words, and future actions.

Bonus Challenge

1. When have I surrendered parts of myself, and to whose authority? What pressured me to surrender? Which parts of myself did I surrender? How did I feel afterward?

2. Why does forgiveness feel so unnatural? Why would God ask me to do something for which I am naturally under-equipped?

3. What do I think of the word "surrender"? What images come to mind? What memories do these images stir up in me? How does God's idea of surrender differ from the way I have understood it?

Week Four
Day 5

The Fragrance of Forgiveness

Come to Christ, who is the living Foundation of Rock upon which God builds; though men have spurned him, he is very precious to God who has chosen him above all others.

And now you have become living building-stones for God's use in building his house. What's more, you are his holy priests; so come to him – [you who are acceptable to him because of Jesus Christ] – and offer to God those things that please him. . . . you have been chosen by God himself – you are priests of the King, you are holy and pure, you are God's very own – all this so that you may show to others how God called you out of the darkness into his wonderful light. Once you were less than nothing; now you are God's own. Once you knew very little of God's kindness; now your very lives have been changed by it. (1 Peter 2:4–5, 9–10, TLB)

When you forgive from a changed heart, you offer up a spiritual sacrifice that pleases God.

Sacrifice is an ancient rite. The Old Testament book of Leviticus describes in great detail the many kinds of offerings and sacrifices that Israel was required to offer to God. Performed only by the priests for the people, sacrifices differed in purpose: *atoning sacrifices* were meant to pay for sins and restore fellowship with God in the community of His people, while *sacrifices of worship* expressed the people's praise, thanksgiving, and devotion to God. Sacrifices that were pleasing and acceptable to God were described as "fragrant" or "a sweet aroma." All Old Testament sacrifices were representative; that is, they were physical expressions of inward devotion and desire to please God, but they could not purify the inner person or make a person righteous before God. Moreover, they were rituals that had to be performed over and over again.

Like the sacrificial animals, Jesus Christ was physically killed, but it was the offering of His sinless life to God that made His death a *spiritual* sacrifice, fragrant to God and sufficient to atone for all our sins for all time.[1] In Christ we are changed from the inside out, and because we are declared righteous and blameless in His name, we each can approach God directly with our offerings of worship. Indeed, as the passage quoted above states, we take on the rights and responsibilities of priests in God's kingdom. We are to offer to God "those things that please him" or, as another translation puts it, "spiritual sacrifices acceptable to God through Jesus Christ."[2]

Jesus ushered in a new era in which we are to worship God not with burnt offerings but "in spirit and truth."[3] Worship that pleases God begins in our hearts and is worked out in our lives. God reveals truth to us through His Word, through Jesus, and through the Holy Spirit He sends to teach and guide us. Our daily activities become acts of worship when they are informed and motivated by our love for God and our desire to live by His standards. The apostle Paul tells us to offer our bodies, our minds, our *lives* to God as spiritual acts of worship.[4]

Spiritual sacrifices please God not only because they help us to mature in our faith but also because they bring God's light into an unsaved world. Unbelievers in our midst see the Father's handprints in what we do; through our acts of obedience to God, others are touched by His love and exposed to truth that can bring hope and salvation into their lives. When we commit our actions to loving God and loving one another, then everything we do—what we speak, what we think, how we serve each other, how we engage physically with the world, what we feed our minds, how we respond to evil, how we pray, how we worship — is a spiritual sacrifice.

Forgiving one another is spiritual sacrifice in the sense that we offer up ourselves in service to God's plan to bring peace and reconciliation to the world. Forgiveness is sacrificial also in the sense that we give up something for the greater good of extending God's redemptive love to the person who injured us:

We worship God with our bodies when we use our words to build up the person who offended us and refuse to gossip about or criticize or ridicule this person; when we use our ears to listen to this person's story; when we restrain our anger and give up physical force, shouting, or violence to control or punish this person; when we use our hands, feet, or other physical gifts to help, comfort, and serve this person.

We worship God with our hearts and minds when we try to see this person through God's eyes; when we give up our bitterness and allow God's love for this person to fill us; when we stop desiring revenge or wishing bad things to happen to this person but instead can earnestly pray for blessings and God's peace to surround and restore him or her; when we remember that God forgave us when we did not deserve it, and we look for ways to extend forgiveness to this person; when we humble ourselves and realize that without Christ we have no righteousness and are no better off than anyone else before God.

We worship God with our lives when we profess our faith and risk the ridicule or hostility of people who think forgiveness is cowardly or foolish; when we give up money or power or position because we forgive our debtors; when we do what is right and just and merciful even when no one sees us but God;

when we treat other people as better than ourselves; when we share our time and personal resources to benefit the person who injured us, even when he or she will not acknowledge the offense.

When you forgive others "from your heart,"[5] you fulfill your priestly function in offering a spiritual sacrifice that brings fragrant pleasure to God. You will also find that your offering brings a sweetness into your own life—peace and healing from the injury of a damaged relationship, a closer walk with God, and the joy of living obediently—as well as into the lives of those who are touched by your forgiving acts.

Today's Fitness Challenge - Day 5

☑ FEED YOUR SOUL: *"The sacrifice acceptable to God is a broken spirit; a broken and contrite heart, O God, you will not despise."*

— Psalm 51:17 (NRSV)

☑ LISTEN TO FORGIVENESS: To forgive one another is a priestly privilege and responsibility.

☑ CHECK YOUR HEART: How might my forgiving bring sweetness into the life of my adversary?

☑ KEEP GOING: With God's help, I will examine my relationships and recognize where God is calling me to offer up spiritual sacrifices.

Bonus Challenge

1. According to 1 Peter 2:9, as a follower of Christ, I belong to a royal priesthood. What makes this priesthood "royal"? What are my duties as a priest? How does my priestly function affect the way I handle relationship problems?

2. How does a spiritual sacrifice differ from a burnt offering? Who benefits from my spiritual sacrifice? Why would God care whether my sacrifice is offered from a heart that is broken and contrite?

3. Why do I take pleasure in those things that keep me from forgiving, such as holding grudges, clinging to my pain and bitterness, or criticizing my adversary to others? Would God

perceive these offerings as "fragrant"? If not, what other adjectives would best describe them?

Week Four
My Fitness Log

☑   *Complete each statement as found in the lesson indicated.* *

1.   It's _____ your job to forgive yourself, but _____. *(DAY 1)*
2.   If we truly could _____ our own sins, then we would have _____ _____ for a Savior. *(DAY 1)*
3.   Inevitably, the _____ that cripples us _____ will show up in our _____. *(DAY 2)*
4.   The more _____ I am with myself, the _____ _____ I find in my neighbor. *(DAY 2)*
5.   Decide whether you would rather ____ _____ or ____ _____. *(DAY 3)*
6.   In a relationship, insisting on being _____ often means _____ _____. *(DAY 3)*
7.   Surrendering your injury to love is _____ to handle your relationship _____ _____. *(DAY 4)*
8.   _____ to love gets easier with _____. *(DAY 4)*
9.   When you _____ from a changed heart, you offer up a _____ _____ that pleases God. *(DAY 5)*
10. To forgive one another is a _____ privilege and _____. *(DAY 5)*

* *See Appendix A for answer key.*

☑   Record the most important lesson you learned this week.

☑   Write a prayer to God. Tell Him truthfully what is in your heart at this stage of your walk and ask Him for what you need to continue.

Week Four
Weekend Workout

Song to God

THE WARM-UP. Read aloud Psalm 28 (ESV):

OF DAVID.
To you, O LORD, I call;
*   my rock, be not deaf to me,*
lest, if you be silent to me,
*   I become like those who go down to the pit.*

Hear the voice of my pleas for mercy,
*   when I cry to you for help,*
when I lift up my hands
*   toward your most holy sanctuary.*

Do not drag me off with the wicked,
*   with the workers of evil,*
who speak peace with their neighbors
*   while evil is in their hearts.*
Give to them according to their work
*   and according to the evil of their deeds;*
give to them according to the work of their hands;
*   render them their due reward.*
Because they do not regard the works of the LORD
*   or the work of his hands,*
he will tear them down and build them up no more.

Blessed be the LORD!

For he has heard the voice of my pleas for mercy.
The LORD *is my strength and my shield;*
   in him my heart trusts, and I am helped;
my heart exults,
   and with my song I give thanks to him.

The LORD *is the strength of his people;*
   he is the saving refuge of his anointed.
Oh, save your people and bless your heritage!
   Be their shepherd and carry them forever.

THE STRETCH. Read the psalm again, but this time silently and prayerfully. Ask the Holy Spirit to pray through the psalm with you.

Which parts of David's song reflect your heart as well? Underline those verses.

Which parts of the song disturb you or feel untrue? Mark those verses with an asterisk.

THE WORKOUT. Psalm 28 is one of the *imprecatory psalms*, or songs in which the psalmist calls down punishment on his enemies. Christians may feel uncomfortable with these psalms because cursing seems to run counter to God's explicit instructions to love our enemies and pray for those who wish us harm. Yet the Psalter—God's prayer book for His people—includes over two dozen psalms that call for God to punish the wicked and vindicate His people.

The imprecatory psalms are more than just a collection of personal gripes. Their calls for God's vengeance conform to very specific ethical themes that elevate them beyond the mere desire of the psalmist to see his enemies suffer:

> The wicked are dishonoring God and refusing to acknowledge His sovereignty.[1]
>
> Wickedness is rampant and severe.[2]
>
> The wicked show no remorse, and their redemption seems unlikely.[3]
>
> God's people are being threatened.[4]
>
> The psalmist calls on God for justice and does not seek revenge on his own.[5]
>
> In the call for divine vengeance is the hope that the ungodly will realize their sin and turn to God.[6]
>
> God's people oppose the powers of evil and long for the establishment of God's kingdom.[7]
>
> Wickedness has been going on for so long that something has to be done about it.[8]
>
> The psalmist calls on God to fulfill His covenant vow to avenge His people for what they suffer.[9]
>
> The wicked seem immune to the psalmist's long-suffering kindness, forgiveness, and peacemaking efforts.[10]
>
> The psalmist is being persecuted because he is a follower of God.[11]
>
> Injustice and sin seem to be winning over justice and righteous living.[12]

Christians need have no qualms about praying anything that was written in the Book of Psalms. Like the psalmists, we sometimes feel blessed and content and at other times feel desperate with fear or sorrow or anger. Praying through an imprecatory psalm puts us in touch with the real feelings of real people who lived before us, who suffered injustice and cruelty as we do at the hands of those who have no respect for God or His laws. Imprecatory psalms teach us to seek God first in the midst of our trials. They acknowledge that sin and injustice in this world are powerful and persuasive and that we must choose again and again to listen for God's voice and seek His ways if we are to be saved from the same fate that God has prepared for those who reject Him and work for the defeat of His kingdom.

Calling down curses on the wicked must be a last resort, reserved for extreme cases of injustice. Like Jesus, we should respond to offenses first with love and kindness, gentleness and forgiveness, always with the hope that our offender's heart will be turned toward God. In some instances, however, there comes a time when justice must be brought in, either by God or by the authorities of power established through government. We can all think of sin so vile or so rampant that justice must be swift and bold. Even in such extreme cases, we never stop praying for the redemption of souls because we have no way of knowing whose hearts God is still wooing. We never forget that we ourselves were saved out of our own wickedness into an inheritance that we did not deserve.

Psalm 28 gives us a good model for working through a personal injustice in a godly way. The following exercise breaks down the psalm into elements that you can use to write your own personal song to God. Follow the table's recommendations to compose your song in the space provided below the table.

Elements of Psalm 28	Adapt Elements Into a Song to God
1 *To you, O LORD, I call; my rock, be not deaf to me, lest, if you be silent to me, I become like those who go down to the pit.* **2** *Hear the voice of my pleas for mercy, when I cry to you for help, when I lift up my hands toward your most holy sanctuary.*	Center your thoughts on God. Ask Him to speak clearly to you, so that you can hear Him. Seek Him earnestly with your voice, your hands, your mind, and your heart. Confess what your life and your fate would be like without Him.
3 *Do not drag me off with the wicked, with the workers of evil, who speak peace with their neighbors while evil is in their hearts.* **4** *Give to them according to their work and according to the evil of their deeds; give to them according to the work of their hands; render them their due reward.* **5** *Because they do not regard the works of the LORD or the work of his hands, he will tear them down and build them up no more.*	Describe everything you know about the offense: who, where, what, when, how, and why. What are your feelings about it? What would you like to see happen to your offender? Be explicit! You will not shock God. Contrast the deeds of your offender with the deeds that please God. Ask God to tear down the sinful patterns in your own life and build you up again in the likeness of Christ.
6 *Blessed be the LORD! For he has heard the voice of my pleas for mercy.* **7** *The LORD is my strength and my shield; in him my heart trusts, and I am helped;*	Pray until God gives you an answer! Your song is not just to express the tumult of your heart but to find God through the tumult. Describe the nature

my heart exults, and with my song I give thanks to him.	of God's answer to you and your feelings about it. Notice if your song has changed.
8 The LORD is the strength of his people; he is the saving refuge of his anointed. 9 Oh, save your people and bless your heritage! Be their shepherd and carry them forever.	Reflect on what it means to be part of the community of God and His anointed heirs. Describe what it means to you to have Christ as your Shepherd.

My Song to God

_____

_____

_____

_____

_____

_____

_____

_____

_____

_____

_____

_____

_____

THE COOL-DOWN. Read through your song to God, asking the Holy Spirit to pray it with you. If the Spirit prompts you, go ahead and add in details to make your song more complete.

Close the session by praying verses 8 and 9 of Psalm 28:

Blessed be the LORD!
   For he has heard the voice of my pleas for mercy.
The LORD *is my strength and my shield;*
   in him my heart trusts, and I am helped;
my heart exults,
   and with my song I give thanks to him.

PART THREE

Maturing in Forgiveness

The Lord GOD is my strength.
He makes me like a deer that does not stumble
so I can walk on the steep mountains.

Habakkuk 3:19, NCV

Week Five

For I have stayed on God's paths;
I have followed his ways and not turned aside.
I have not departed from his commands,
but have treasured his words more than daily food. (Job 23:11-12, NLT)

Week Five
Day 1

Ten Habits of Forgiveness

Let everything you say be good and helpful, so that your words will be an encouragement to those who hear them.

And do not bring sorrow to God's Holy Spirit by the way you live. Remember, he has identified you as his own, guaranteeing that you will be saved on the day of redemption.

Get rid of all bitterness, rage, anger, harsh words, and slander, as well as all types of evil behavior. Instead, be kind to each other, tenderhearted, forgiving one another, just as God through Christ has forgiven you. (Ephesians 4:29-32, NLT)

Forgiveness becomes a lifestyle as you apply kingdom values to your daily habits.

You've made it to the final week of your training—good for you! By now, you are familiar with the principles of forgiveness and the qualities of a forgiving lifestyle. You have learned as well that, for the spiritually fit, forgiving is not an option but a requirement: "Bear with one another and, if anyone has a complaint against another, forgive each other; just as the Lord has forgiven you, so you also must forgive."[1] Scripture makes it clear that you cannot mature in your faith unless you mature in your ability to forgive as well.

Essential to any fitness training is the adoption of new habits to replace those that might keep you from achieving your goals. To become a more forgiving person, you must examine your characteristic responses to conflict and question whether they are pleasing to God. Habits are so quick and reflexive that you might feel you have no control over them. The truth is, habits are learned behaviors that can be unlearned; by deliberately exposing them, you can replace them with new behaviors that will help you to align yourself with God's purpose for you.

Listed below are ten habits of forgiveness that will help you to achieve and maintain a high level of spiritual fitness.

(1) Forgive what you can.

Blessed is he whose transgressions are forgiven, whose sins are covered.[2]

Forgiveness is a process that can unfold quickly or, as in a case of deep wounding, very slowly and with difficulty. With God's help, you can begin to "bless and not curse" your offender immediately, even while the Spirit is still working to change your heart. If you are hurt and angry, perhaps all you can manage today is to keep yourself from gossiping or saying harsh things about the person who hurt you. Decide where you can start to forgive and then, with God's help, do it. Be patient but resolved to daily surrender your conflict to God and allow the Spirit to refine and heal you.

(2) Seek forgiveness from others.

So when you offer your gift to God at the altar, and you remember that your brother or sister has something against you, leave your gift there at the altar. Go and make peace with that person, and then come and offer your gift.[3]

We are more likely to forgive others when we recognize our kinship with them as helpless sinners before God. None of us is righteous; we each sin against our neighbors and do things we later wish we hadn't done. The experience of seeking and accepting forgiveness from someone you have offended both humbles and empowers you to similarly extend compassion when someone else needs your forgiveness.

(3) Pray for your offender.

You're familiar with the old written law, 'Love your friend,' and its unwritten companion, 'Hate your enemy.' I'm challenging that. I'm telling you to love your enemies. Let them bring out the best in you, not the worst. When someone gives you a hard time, respond with the energies of prayer, for then you are working out of your true selves, your God-created selves.[4]

Prayer is essential to changing your heart toward your offender. In the sanctuary of God's presence, His Spirit comforts and reassures you, and here you can begin to surrender your anger and pain over your wounding. Through the practice of prayer, you open yourself to the healing resources you need to forgive: compassion, God's perspective and purpose, patience, faith in God's sovereignty, hope, joy, and all the good fruit of the Spirit.[5]

(4) Speak carefully.

Reckless words pierce like a sword, but the tongue of the wise brings healing.[6]

A brother who has been insulted is harder to win back than a walled city, and arguments separate people like the barred gates of a palace.[7]

We all know how words can hurt. We also know how gracious, respectful words can heal. The language of forgiveness is gentle, loving, patient, and kindly. Forgiveness always seeks to heal and build up rather than to attack and tear down. Although you cannot control how the other person will respond, you can cultivate the habit of speaking in a tone and language that honor God.

(5) Encourage peacemaking.

For God in all his fullness was pleased to live in Christ, and through him God reconciled everything to himself. He made peace with everything in heaven and on earth by means of Christ's blood on the cross.[8]

Followers of Christ are called to peacemaking because restoring broken relationships is so close to God's loving heart. To bring peace into your community is to challenge the devil's hold on people's hearts and offer kingdom solutions to conflicts. When you retaliate with love instead of hatred and with mercy instead of condemnation, you make visible to the world the very nature of your heavenly Father.

(6) Commit to honesty.

Teach me, and I will be quiet; show me where I have been wrong. How painful are honest words![9]

Truth provides the only solid ground for rebuilding a damaged relationship. Refusing to acknowledge the truth about a hurtful event may seem protective at first but in the long run only postpones healing. A process of acknowledging the hurt, assessing loss, and properly assigning blame, whether yours or the other person's, promotes recovery when it's done with patience and gentleness and an earnest desire to repair the damage and move the relationship forward.

(7) Humble yourself.

All of you must clothe yourselves with humility in your dealings with one another, for "God opposes the proud, but gives grace to the humble."[10]

Those with humble hearts are blessed because they understand the value of forgiveness. The proud, on the other hand, have no use for either giving or receiving mercy. God's grace is available to all but can fill only those who are emptied of their own sense of importance and self-sufficiency. The habit of pride will prevent you from receiving God's forgiveness and extending merciful compassion to others.

(8) Imitate Christ.

But [Christ Jesus] made himself nothing, taking the very nature of a servant, and being made in human likeness.[11]

As followers of Christ, we bring honor to God by serving one another in joy, humility, and love. Jesus showed us by example that we demonstrate love when we give of ourselves and our possessions to serve each other's needs. An important habit of forgiveness is to look through the offense and ask, What can I do to ease the suffering of this person who hurt me?

(9) Love because God loves.

Dear friends, we should love each other, because love comes from God. Everyone who loves has become God's child and knows God. Whoever does not love does not know God, because God is love.[12]

Our nature can become more loving only through the gift of God's grace. We cannot "make" ourselves more loving, but as we open ourselves to be filled by God, we in turn can bless and comfort others with the love He gives us. Forgiving those who offend you means loving them with the graceful and holy love that flows through you from God's own heart.

(10) Depend on God.

I am the vine, and you are the branches. If any remain in me and I remain in them, they produce much fruit. But without me they can do nothing.[13]

God doesn't intend for you to forgive all on your own. Whatever God asks you to do, depend upon Him to give you the strength and the grace to do it. Forgiving your enemies is a sacred task that has spiritual consequences, both for you and for your enemies. Obey God by returning good for the evil you receive, and trust in His sovereign authority to judge.

Today's Fitness Challenge - Day 1

☑ FEED YOUR SOUL: *"One of the marks of spiritual maturity is the quiet confidence that God is in control...without the need to understand why he does what he does."*
—Charles R. Swindoll, author

☑ LISTEN TO FORGIVENESS: A forgiving heart grows stronger with exercise.

☑ CHECK YOUR HEART: Which habit(s) of forgiveness have I already begun to practice?

☑ KEEP GOING: With God's help, I will replace harmful habits with the habits of a forgiving lifestyle.

Bonus Challenge

1. Which habits of forgiveness present the greatest challenge to me? What habits of mine must I give up in order to practice these new habits?

2. Is it easier for me to extend forgiveness to others or to seek forgiveness from others? How was forgiveness modeled in the home where I grew up?

3. Why is honesty so important in forgiving? How have I been less than honest in my conflicts with others? How has the dishonesty of others hindered my ability to forgive and be reconciled?

Week Five
Day 2

Family Thorns

"Listen! A farmer went out to sow his seed. As he was scattering the seed, some fell along the path, and the birds came and ate it up. Some fell on rocky places, where it did not have much soil. It sprang up quickly, because the soil was shallow. But when the sun came up, the plants were scorched, and they withered because they had no root. Other seed fell among thorns, which grew up and choked the plants, so that they did not bear grain. Still other seed fell on good soil. It came up, grew and produced a crop, multiplying thirty, sixty, or even a hundred times."

Then Jesus said, "He who has ears to hear, let him hear." (Mark 4:3-9)

Family wounds are among the most difficult to heal and to forgive.

We can borrow from Jesus' agrarian theme and regard a family as a field in which members put down roots and grow to maturity. According to His illustration, the nature of the soil is critical to the success of the crop. If the soil is to promote optimum growth, it must have two important characteristics: (a) it must be deep enough for a plant to put down strong roots that can both draw in water and nutrients and also anchor itself to stand against harsh weather conditions such as wind, flood, heat, or fire; and (b) it must be wholesome, free from contamination and from thorn and weed infestation. Human families who provide healthy, nurturing environments seem to offer their members the best chance for strong roots and abundant, upright growth.

Realistically, however, no family provides an environment that is completely healthy, nurturing, and free from the corrupting influence of sin. All families fail their members, some more than others and in different ways. Unfulfilled needs, jealousies, and disputes over expectations contaminate the family soil, while secrets, betrayals, and sometimes outright abuse infest family plantings and strangle growth. No family is immune to these destructive influences; anyone who has been raised in a family readily understands how family wounds can sting like nettles and linger, festering into a deep, angry sorrow.

Thorny family conflicts are among the most painful and the most difficult to forgive. Nevertheless, if we want to live a life of peace and joy, if we want to be free to follow in Christ's footsteps without reservation, then we *must* expose and heal these wounds because they never leave us on their own. Even if a conflict happened years ago, and we have forgotten the particulars of the event, our feelings about it persist—in our dreams, in our attitudes about trust and hope and loyalty, and in our ability to accept ourselves, to love God, or to sustain nurturing adult relationships. Today's conflict with a spouse or coworker or child or friend may be rooted in a long-ago conflict with a family member that was never resolved. Consequently, healing our wounds of long ago help us to resolve today's conflicts as well. In healing the tender areas of our lives, we become less prone to take offense and more inclined to let go of resentments before they build up.

How Our Families Hurt Us

Most quarrels with people in general, not just with family members, begin with unmet expectations. We expect certain behaviors or words or services from people, and when they do not oblige us, we feel wronged. Our disappointments within families become especially painful when our expectations arise from a list of needs that we look to our families to satisfy. When families do not meet these needs, our resentment can be layered over with doubts about our self-worth and our lovability — "If they *cared* about me, if I were *valuable* to them, then they would surely meet my needs!"

Listed below is a sampling of what we typically need and expect from our families:

A name; identity with the family.
Wisdom, advice, and practical information.
A sense of significance — "I matter."
Encouragement.
Unconditional love; affection.
Strength in numbers — "we have your back."
Friendship.
Realistic feedback about who I am.
Respect.
Continuity with past generations.
Loyalty.
Shared past, present, and future.
Helpful role models.
Worldview; moral code; religion.
Assurance of belonging.
Affirmation of my life and my choices.

Families may fail to meet these basic needs through either *acts of omission* or *acts of malice*. An act of omission is a failure to act in a way that benefits another. The parent who withholds affection, the mother who refuses to acknowledge her daughter's molestation, or the adult sibling who never returns phone calls is each committing an act of omission. In various ways these people fail to meet the specific needs of their family members. Despite the seeming passivity of the wounding, such wounds can nevertheless hurt very deeply. Such acts of omission are difficult to expose and heal when the wounding is subtle and not easily identified as the person's source of pain. For example, neglected children may grow up ashamed of their legitimate needs and as adults be reluctant to ask for what they need in caring relationships; they don't realize that their shame is rooted in an absence of attention from childhood caretakers.

In contrast, an act of malice is a deliberate attempt to harm another. Abuse of any kind — physical, sexual, emotional, verbal, or psychological — aimed at a family member of any age is an act of malice. The father who beats his children into submission, the caretaking daughter who treats her elderly mother harshly, or the brother who constantly tells his younger brother that he is stupid and clumsy are all committing acts of malice. Such acts are by nature painful and destructive, but when they occur within families, they can be devastating — spirits are crushed, family relationships are crippled, and individuals are driven into destructive lifestyles, sometimes even suicide. Many adults who are socially maladjusted can recount childhood episodes of deliberate wounding by the very people who were supposed to care for them. Depression, fears and phobias, addictions, and abuse of one's own children can very often be traced to acts of malice committed in the confusing, powerless environment of one's own childhood.

Why Our Families Hurt Us

On the surface it makes no sense that family members would hurt one another. Ideally, our families should provide the one safe place where we can be assured of love and support. The

Bible tells us, however, that even from the beginning families have engaged in selfish, brutal, and sometimes murderous conflict—Cain killed his brother, Abel; Joseph's brothers sold him into slavery and lied to their father about it; King David's son Amnon raped his half-sister Tamar; Absalom conspired to take the throne away from his father. Even Jesus' own brothers ridiculed Him in public.[1]

In the clutches of sin, contemporary families continue to hurt one another—a raging father humiliates his son in the same way that his own father humiliated him; a narcissistic mother cripples her daughter's spirit with constant berating; a jealous teenager abuses her handicapped sister for stealing the family's attention. Mental illness, emotional immaturity, crippled self-esteem, ignorance, or deliberate desire to do evil—we can only guess at the reasons why families choke each other with stinging nettles and deadly thorns. Although God alone can know a person's heart, we must nonetheless bear the burden of family wounds, whatever their cause, and find a way to move beyond them.

How to Forgive Our Families

The first step in forgiving your family is to accept God's invitation to transplant you into the healthy soil of His kingdom family: "Both the one who makes people holy and those who are made holy are of the same family. So Jesus is not ashamed to call them brothers and sisters."[2] In the Father's field, you can drink in living water to your heart's content and never be thirsty again.[3] The soil is pure and wholesome; there are no weeds to compete for nutrients and no thorns to strangle you and keep you small and puny. Your roots can grow deep and strong, able to stand against whatever life sends your way. And the glory of God gives light always, replacing the sun, giving you all you need to thrive and mature.[4]

The second step in forgiving your family is to surrender your wounds to God. This means giving up your authority to judge, condemn, and punish the family members who hurt you. As God's child, you are free to surrender your wounds to Him because you no longer look to your earthly family to meet your basic needs — your heavenly Father has promised to meet every need you have and in ways that are more satisfying and nurturing than your human family could ever supply.[5] You no longer have reason to fear or resent your family because you are no longer subject to their rules. As an heir in God's kingdom, you can leave judgment to Him and to the legal authority of government He has established for your benefit and protection.[6]

The third step in forgiving your family is to ask God to give you a pure heart, a good conscience, and a sincere faith.[7] These three elements of Christian integrity will protect you from the little niggling sins that can pull you back into resentful patterns of thought and behavior. They pave the way for forgiveness and provide you with resources you need to take the final step.

The final step in forgiving your family is to ask God for a healing vision and the love to forgive them. You won't find these miracles within yourself or learn them from a book; they are gifts of the Spirit. Remember that God's thoughts and ways are higher and truer than human thoughts and ways.[8] You must borrow God's insight into your family wounds, laying aside all blame and accusations, and adopt His healing vision for each family member. Only God can replace your pain with a love so real and deep that you truly long to see your family transplanted into healthy soil and released, as you were, from the tangles and thorns of unfinished conflict.

It is important to realize that you are not responsible for your family's healing, nor can you guarantee peace in the midst of family conflict. Your offer of forgiveness may be rejected, your demonstrations of love rebuffed. Your joy in belonging to God's kingdom may antagonize rather than comfort your family. Jesus warned His disciples, "I have told you these things, so that in me you may have peace. In this world you will have trouble. But take heart! I have overcome the world."[9] Only Christ has the power to bring absolute and everlasting peace to human conflict. Yet He promises that *you* can have this perfect peace *in Him*, right now and forever. Your business is to put down strong roots in the good soil God has given you and to grow in faith, a good conscience, and a pure heart. You can forgive your family and take joy in that miracle, no matter how your family responds.

Today's Fitness Challenge - Day 2

☑ FEED YOUR SOUL: *"And you, son of man, do not be afraid of them or their words. Do not be afraid, though briers and thorns are all around you and you live among scorpions. Do not be afraid of what they say or be terrified by them, though they are a rebellious house."*

—Ezekiel 2:6

☑ LISTEN TO FORGIVENESS: I need God's kingdom family to help me forgive my human family.

☑ CHECK YOUR HEART: Which of my needs has my family been unable or unwilling to meet?

☑ KEEP GOING: With God's help, I will anchor myself in the good soil of God's kingdom family and learn His family rules.

Bonus Challenge

1. Why does God allow our families to hurt us? How did family thorns affect my growing up? Which thorns still hurt me?

2. In what ways have I been a thorn in my family? Who was hurt by my thorny actions? What prompted me to act that way?

3. How can "a pure heart, a good conscience, and a sincere faith" help me to forgive?

Week Five
Day 3

Facing Our Flaws

Consider it a sheer gift, friends, when tests and challenges come at you from all sides. You know that under pressure, your faith-life is forced into the open and shows its true colors. So don't try to get out of anything prematurely. Let it do its work so you become mature and well-developed, not deficient in any way.

If you don't know what you're doing, pray to the Father. He loves to help. You'll get his help, and won't be condescended to when you ask for it. Ask boldly, believingly, without a second thought. People who "worry their prayers" are like wind-whipped waves. Don't think you're going to get anything from the Master that way, adrift at sea, keeping all your options open.

Don't let anyone under pressure to give in to evil say, "God is trying to trip me up." God is impervious to evil, and puts evil in no one's way. The temptation to give in to evil comes from us and only us. We have no one to blame but the leering, seducing flare-up of our own lust. Lust gets pregnant, and has a baby: sin! Sin grows up to adulthood, and becomes a real killer.

So, my very dear friends, don't get thrown off course. Every desirable and beneficial gift comes out of heaven. The gifts are rivers of light cascading down from the Father of Light. There is nothing deceitful in God, nothing two-faced, nothing fickle. He brought us to life using the true Word, showing us off as the crown of all his creatures. (James 1:2-8, 13-18, MSG)

Quarrels and conflicts can be useful because they expose our character flaws.

A flaw is an imperfection that detracts from the whole or a deficiency that hinders usefulness or effectiveness. Flaws in our Christian character are the weak points where we are most tempted to sin and most likely to turn away from God, where we put our trust in old habits and allow fear or anger or pride to dictate our behaviors. Our flaws diminish our integrity and our ability to follow in Christ's footsteps. Calamity, trauma, financial pressure, persecution, interpersonal conflict, physical ailments, and other stressors test us for these weak points.

A flaw is not the same as sin. To sin is to willfully turn our backs on God and His laws and go our own way. Sinning results in our estrangement from God and also from others — every quarrel and conflict can be traced to sin as its root cause.[1] But flaws do not cause quarrels. When I say, "I have a short temper," it means that I have a weakness that can get me into trouble if I allow it to control me. My *flaw* is the urgent pull I feel to react with quick and destructive anger when I feel threatened; my *sin* is choosing to submit to that pull and unleash my anger.

When we are in the habit of letting our flaws control us, we may not realize that we do in fact choose to sin. My quick temper may feel beyond my conscious control, but that's only my habit speaking. To sin is always my choice. Habits can form around any flaw and prime us to fall quickly into a sinful response to others' words or actions almost before we realize what we are doing; as quickly as some will respond with anger, others will respond with anxiety, fear, shame, criticism, violence, withdrawal, defensiveness, ridicule, contempt, retaliation...the list goes on. The important point is that sinning is the second step in a very quick process; feeling the temptation to sin is the first step.

There is nothing inherently shameful about having flaws. We each have them, and God has promised to send His Spirit to help us with them.[2] In fact, God uses our weaknesses as entry points into our lives so that we may experience His presence and His power and give witness of Him to others.[3] Having our weaknesses exposed through trials and conflicts gives us choices: either we can continue to give in to our weaknesses and let them lead us away from God, or we can confess them and ask God to give us His strength to fight their influence over us. Surrendering these vulnerable areas of our lives to God's control opens us to the refining of our character by the Holy Spirit into a likeness of Christ, which is the joyous goal of every believer.

The table below contrasts the choices we can make in the face of conflict:

When my flaws control me...	When God controls my flaws...
I exaggerate my adversary's flaws and my virtues.	I remember that no one is righteous before God.[4]
My wound becomes too important, dominating my thoughts and spoiling my life.	My wound seems of small importance in the light of eternity and God's Kingdom.[5]
I am crushed by the hardship of a conflict.	I am made strong by the testing of my character.[6]
I do not want my flaws exposed.	I am eager for God to examine me.[7]
I wish harm and discomfort on my adversary.	I wish my adversary to be comforted as I have been comforted.[8]

I allow the conflict to lead me away from God.	I allow the conflict to lead me closer to God.[9]
My woundedness makes me selfish and suspicious.	My woundedness inspires me to be generous.[10]
I am surprised by my hardships, and I resent them.	I expect hardships, and I welcome their refining effects.[11]
I do what I think will get the results I want.	I follow God's laws to get the results He values.[12]
I nurse my grudges and refuse to forgive.	I remember how God forgave me while I was still His enemy.[13]

Finally, the introductory Scripture passage for this chapter offers four imperatives to help you surrender your flaws to God's control:

"Consider it a sheer gift, friends, when tests and challenges come at you from all sides." James urges you to celebrate not the pain and hardship of a conflict but rather the fresh opportunity for God to work a miracle in your life. Seize His gift of becoming aware of your flaws and His promise to help you deal with them.

"If you don't know what you're doing, pray to the Father." Don't be ashamed to confess your weaknesses to God and ask for help. He is never condescending; furthermore, He has promised to provide a way out of temptation "so that you can stand up under it."[14]

"Don't let anyone under pressure to give in to evil say,

'**God is trying to trip me up.**'" Learn to recognize your flaws and the particular ways in which you are tempted to sin. Take responsibility for the ways in which your sins have contributed to the conflicts in your life.

"**Don't get thrown off course.**" Don't let your flaws tempt you to stop walking with forgiveness. Realize that the refining of your character is a process that takes time. You will make mistakes, but you have a Father who loves you and longs to give you good gifts that will last for all eternity. Trust God and stay the course.

Today's Fitness Challenge - Day 3

☑ FEED YOUR SOUL: *"Look closely at yourselves. Test yourselves to see if you are living in the faith."*
— 2 Corinthians 13:5 (NCV)

☑ LISTEN TO FORGIVENESS: It is the recognition of our flaws, not our perfections, that compels us to forgive one another.

☑ CHECK YOUR HEART: What is my biggest flaw, and what is the sin it pulls me into?

☑ KEEP GOING: With God's help, I will view conflict as a rich source of information about my character strengths and flaws.

Bonus Challenge

1. In what instances have I been at least partly responsible for a quarrel? What sin(s) of mine contributed to the conflict?

2. How do I feel about being described as "flawed"? How did my family deal with its flawed members? Has God ever manifested His presence or power through a weakness of mine?

3. Which flaws do I find most offensive in others? in myself? What is the difference between a flaw and a sin? How can understanding this difference help me to forgive?

Week Five
Day 4

Forgiving the Unrepentant

Two others, both criminals, were taken along with him for execution.

When they got to the place called Skull Hill, they crucified him, along with the criminals, one on his right, the other on his left.

Jesus prayed, "Father, forgive them; they don't know what they're doing."

Dividing up his clothes, they threw dice for them. The people stood there staring at Jesus, and the ringleaders made faces, taunting, "He saved others. Let's see him save himself! The Messiah of God — ha! The Chosen — ha!"

The soldiers also came up and poked fun at him, making a game of it. They toasted him with sour wine: "So you're King of the Jews! Save yourself!" (Luke 23:32-37, MSG)

Is it possible to forgive and reconcile with an unrepentant offender?

Throughout the Bible God repeatedly stresses the importance of mending broken relationships, both with Himself and with other people. Forgiveness is vital because it removes barriers to reconciliation and prepares us for healing. In a world where sin is an unfortunate reality, forgiveness is an indispensable antidote for relationship ills.

Forgiving is easiest when the offense is minor; it becomes more difficult as our losses increase and/or a personal trust is betrayed. Still, if our offender realizes his guilt and repents, God expects us to forgive him: "If your brother sins, rebuke him, and if he repents, forgive him. If he sins against you seven times a day, and seven times comes back to you and says, 'I repent,' forgive him."[1]

The Bible is not as clear about forgiving the offender who will not admit fault. Nowhere does it say, "You shall forgive the unrepentant sinner who commits crimes and then shrugs off accusations of wrongdoing." So then, what are we to do about the offender who refuses to apologize? Is repentance a requirement before we can forgive?

Although there is no direct command to forgive the unrepentant, the Bible records several instances where the forgiver does not wait for an expression of repentance:

Joseph revealed his identity to his brothers and, before they could respond, forgave them for kidnapping him, selling him into slavery, and lying to their father about his death.[2]

The father forgave his prodigal son on sight before he knew why his son had returned home.[3]

Jesus forgave an adulterous woman who was brought before Him for judgment but never asked Him for mercy.[4]

Jesus forgave a paralytic man who was brought to Him for healing, although the man did not ask to be forgiven.[5]

Jesus forgave His disciples, and especially Peter, for denying and deserting Him on the night He was arrested.[6]

From the cross, Jesus asked the Father to forgive the soldiers and religious leaders and ordinary people who were torturing and mocking Him. He prayed not silently, in the quiet of His heart, but with breath that cost Him as the crucifixion squeezed the air from His lungs in slow suffocation. He prayed for His unrepentant offenders in a voice loud enough for them to hear: "Father, forgive them; they don't know what they're doing."

Why would Jesus make such an effort to forgive offensive, unapologetic mockers within their hearing? The answer is, Jesus forgave them for the same reason He did everything else — He was on earth to do the Father's will.[7] In fact, He was suffering on a cross at that very moment because the Father's will was to woo unrepentant sinners back into relationship with Him. Through the death and resurrection of Jesus, God made unfathomable grace available to each of us while we were still His enemies — rebellious, godless, and dead in our sins.[8]

We who claim to live by the Spirit are also called to forgive our enemies, even the arrogant, unrepentant people who nevertheless are so loved by God that He wants to use *us* to woo them into His kingdom. The work of forgiving these people is difficult, even impossible without God's help. Nevertheless, when we are obedient and attentive to the Spirit, God moves through our hearts, refining and healing us in profound ways that we could never otherwise experience.

If, then, we commit ourselves to forgiving, how do we go about it? The Bible does give us several pointers on how to work through conflict with an uncooperative offender.

Pray. *Always* begin with prayer! Pray in four steps:

(1) Tell God exactly what you think about the situation, how you feel, and what you think ought to be done about it. Be honest; be detailed. Get all your feelings out into the open.

(2) Ask God to help you see through your biases, your exaggerations, your false assumptions, and anything else that distorts your perception of the offense, your offender, or yourself. God has been with you through the entire experience; He knows all the details. You may want to write down what you

learn as God helps you refocus your memory and your understanding of what happened.

(3) Pray as Jesus did in the garden just before His arrest: "Take this cup from me. Yet not what I will, but what you will."[9] Ask God to take your will and transform it into a likeness of His own. Ask Him for the will to forgive and for the love you will need to motivate you. Ask for wisdom, for strength, for whatever you need to follow the Spirit's leading with joyful obedience.

(4) Ask God for His peace, which "transcends all understanding," to guard your mind and your heart against further anguish and bitterness.[10] Ask for peace and comfort right now, today, and every day on your journey of forgiving.

Ground your behaviors in love. No matter how your offender responds to you, don't repay evil for evil or retaliate with insults. Instead, try to be a blessing, which is what God has called you to do.[11] The Bible tells us to feed a hungry enemy and give him water to drink when he is thirsty.[12] By looking past the offense into the needy heart of your offender, you begin to see what God sees, and you become an agent of His love when you minister to those needs. Who knows, but God may use your compassion to bring your unrepentant offender to repentance. Pray for your offender, and pray for the grace to wish him the best.

Hold your offender accountable. Forgiveness is not a free pass to continue offensive or destructive behaviors. Forgiveness that is motivated by love always asserts the truth in the hope that the offender will recognize and give up the hurtful behavior. Your forgiving does not *enable*; that is, it does not encourage the offender to continue sinning by your overlooking, denying, excusing, or lying to cover up the offensive behavior. On the contrary, your loving concern for the spiritual well-being of the other person compels you to be honest about the reality of the sinful behavior and to do all you can to help the other person overcome it.[13]

Submit to God's system of justice. God is loving and is also just. These two attributes are not mutually exclusive; in fact, God's loving nature *motivates* His justice as He advocates for goodness and truth and hates the evil that causes suffering and horror and destruction. We, too, have an innate sense of justice, and when someone sins against us, we instinctively want to retaliate to "balance the scales." Unlike God's justice, however, ours is oriented toward self-preservation and limited by our sin nature. God's justice looks out for the best interests of both you and your offender, as well as the people in community with you. In matters where sinful behavior is serious enough to require discipline, God has established a system for addressing sin within the believing community, as described in Matthew 18:15-17 — first approaching the unrepentant offender privately, by yourself, and gradually involving others as necessary, all in the hope of promoting repentance in the offender while protecting others who might be harmed by the sin. God has also given our government systems the authority and means to discipline and punish those who harm innocent people. Even when you have forgiven your offender, submitting your case to the court system may be a necessary act of love and prudence to protect the innocent and to encourage your offender to examine himself and repent.

Give up your personal desire for revenge. "Do not take revenge, my friends, but leave room for God's wrath, for it is written: 'It is mine to avenge; I will repay,' says the Lord."[14] God's wrath — His holy and righteous anger — is a serious and fearful thing. All Scripture points ahead to a day of judgment, when God's wrath will be unleashed against all those who reject truth and follow evil.[15] Sometimes, though, we are impatient; we feel like the psalmist who wrote:

How long, O LORD?
  How long will the wicked be allowed to gloat?
How long will they speak with arrogance?
  How long will these evil people boast?
They crush your people, LORD,
  hurting those you claim as your own.[16]

From our human perspective, God may seem distant and either impotent or uncaring in dealing with the unrepentant offenders who torment us. And that's exactly why we must give up our personal desire for revenge: our perspective is small and self-focused; our knowledge is limited and distorted. God speaks the truth when He says, "It is mine to avenge; I will repay." God takes personally the acts of evildoers and blasphemers and the arrogant who mock Him and persecute His people. As much as God loves His creation, He hates the sin and wickedness that corrupt it, and He has His own plans for revenge.

When you give up your right to revenge, you are asserting your belief that God is sovereign, is fully engaged in His creation, and knows exactly what He is doing, even if you don't understand it: "'For my thoughts are not your thoughts, neither are your ways my ways,' declares the LORD. 'As the heavens are higher than the earth, so are my ways higher than your ways and my thoughts than your thoughts.'"[17] God does not ignore your suffering, but He will act in exactly the way He desires and in His own timing. Moreover, His action may surprise and even disappoint you — instead of bringing calamity to your offender, He might bring prosperity; instead of a curse, a blessing; instead of condemnation, salvation and eternal reward.

Finally, although it is possible for you to forgive, you cannot reconcile your relationship with those who refuse to acknowledge their hurtful behavior. Reconciliation requires a mutual effort. Trust, essential to any healthy relationship, cannot be reestablished with an offender who continues to sin without remorse. Even without reconciliation, however, forgiving the unrepentant frees you to live in peace without bitterness and thoughts of personal revenge, and it clears a path to reconciliation should that day come when your offender does experience remorse. Forgiveness helps you to live with spiritual integrity by removing whatever might keep you from knowing and enjoying God's presence in your life. Moreover, as God's light shines through your words and actions, it may touch the need in your offender's heart, to expose sin and stir up a desire to repent.

Today's Fitness Challenge - Day 4

☑ FEED YOUR SOUL: *"If it is possible, as far as it depends on you, live at peace with everyone."*

— Romans 12:18

☑ LISTEN TO FORGIVENESS: Forgiving brings God's light into dark places.

☑ CHECK YOUR HEART: What is the worst offense I have suffered where my offender refused to take responsibility?

☑ KEEP GOING: With God's help, I will clear a path to reconciliation with my unrepentant offender and leave the rest in God's hands.

Bonus Challenge

1. Why is it easier to forgive someone who will admit responsibility for a transgression than someone who refuses to be sorry?

2. Has there been an instance when my offender admitted guilt, repented, and apologized to me? How did I respond? How would our relationship be different today if this person had not repented and asked for forgiveness?

3. What makes it difficult for me to acknowledge my guilt to someone I've hurt and ask for forgiveness? What could this person do that would in any way help me to repent?

Week Five
Day 5

Beyond Blame

Therefore, since we are surrounded by such a huge crowd of witnesses to the life of faith, let us strip off every weight that slows us down, especially the sin that so easily trips us up. And let us run with endurance the race God has set before us. We do this by keeping our eyes on Jesus, the champion who initiates and perfects our faith. Because of the joy awaiting him, he endured the cross, disregarding its shame. Now he is seated in the place of honor beside God's throne. Think of all the hostility he endured from sinful people; then you won't become weary and give up. After all, you have not yet given your lives in your struggle against sin.

And have you forgotten the encouraging words God spoke to you as his children? He said,

> *"My child, don't make light of the LORD's discipline,*
> *and don't give up when he corrects you.*
> *For the LORD disciplines those he loves,*
> *and he punishes each one he accepts as his child."*

As you endure this divine discipline, remember God is treating you as his own children....God's discipline is always good for us, so that we might share in his holiness. No discipline is enjoyable while it is happening — it's painful! But afterward there will be a peaceful harvest of right living for those who are trained in this way.

So take a new grip with your tired hands and strengthen your weak knees. Mark out a straight path for your feet so that those who are weak and lame will not fall but become strong. (Hebrews 12:1-7, 10-13, NLT)

Blame is a weight that slows you down in the race God has set before you.

Suffering and loss are inescapable facts of our earthly existence. For every person, life proceeds by letting go of what is past or what is no longer needed so that we can take hold of what lies in the future. For example, the very act of maturing requires that we accept the loss of our younger self in order to achieve our older self. Some losses seem minor, and others can be so painful that our passage into the future is slow and tortuous. The deep sadness of losing a loved one to death, a marriage to divorce, or our health to disease or disability challenges our capacity to cope and requires the healing work of grief to help us move forward.

Sometimes our suffering in loss is compounded by our belief that the loss was *unjust*. Our pain is magnified because we are convinced that our suffering was not inevitable but rather imposed by someone's unfair action: our identity is stolen, a business partner cheats us, a close friend is killed by a drunk driver. In such cases, we come to view our loss as the consequence of an *offense* by someone who took advantage of our human vulnerability. We have been robbed not only of someone or something that we valued but also of a future to which we felt entitled. We feel cheated, we feel violated, and we look for someone to blame.

The Weight That Slows You Down

Blaming is a powerful method of refocusing our negative emotions and attentions on the person whom we hold responsible for our misery. Blaming can occur so quickly and so instinctively that it feels inherently just. The need to blame is part of our human nature; even young children know how to point an accusing finger. Assigning blame feels good because it helps us to regain a sense of control in a situation that has caught us off guard and made us to feel helpless and weak. It gives us a target for our pain and justification for our outrage.

Perhaps surprisingly, affixing blame is an important and necessary step in the process of forgiving. If we want to make sense of what happened and give some meaning to our loss, then we must understand the nature of the offense and who was responsible. Accurately assigning blame can be especially helpful for those who have taken unwarranted blame upon themselves, such as adult survivors of childhood abuse or victims of violation by a domestic partner, an employer, a pastor, or a therapist. Shifting the blame to where it belongs frees the victim to begin healing from the injury. It may also be a first step in seeking justice through the court system, protecting oneself and others from further abuse, and getting treatment for the perpetrator.

Helpful blame, however, is by nature transitory. Blaming is useful only for clarification and makes a poor lifestyle. When we become too attached to our need to blame, then we invest our thoughts and energy into obsessing about our offender instead of preparing ourselves to accept our loss and move on. Excessive blaming undermines our ability to recover from an injury:

Blaming fuels negative emotions, of which the apostle Paul warns us: "Get rid of all bitterness, rage and anger, brawling and slander, along with every form of malice."[1]

Blaming tends to oversimplify the wounding event, ignoring contributing factors and demonizing the offender.

Blaming allows the strong emotions of anger and resentment to mask deeper emotions, such as fear, guilt, sorrow, or shame.

Blaming keeps us locked in the past and prevents the natural grieving process from moving us through our loss into recovery.

Blaming keeps us distant from our offender and prevents us from extending compassion.

Blaming fosters hatred, which keeps us from walking in the light of Christ.[2]

Blaming tempts us to seek revenge.

Excessive blaming takes us away from God and from the resources we need to heal from our loss. It is a sin that weights us down and must be stripped off before we can follow the Spirit's leading into the future God has planned for us.

Running the Race God Has Set Before You

If you are committed to living in faithful obedience to God and following Christ's example, then at some point you must surrender to God your right to blaming. In doing so, you invite the Spirit to correct your understanding of your loss, your offender, and yourself.

Your loss. The event that precipitated your loss is redefined in the light of God's sovereignty. The wounding seems less random and unfair as you remember that God "works out everything in conformity with the purpose of his will, in order that we, who were the first to hope in Christ, might be for the praise of his glory."[3] Instead of meaningless hardship, your experience is recast as a testing that God lovingly uses to develop in you a faith that will help you persevere and grow your Christian character to maturity.[4]

Your offender. The person whose behavior caused your loss is reevaluated without prejudice and from God's perspective.

The truth is, your offender is no less righteous than you are before God: "There is no difference, for all have sinned and fall short of the glory of God."[5] Furthermore, God desires not to condemn your offender but to extend the same offer of love and redemption that He extended to you.[6] The sinful behavior of this person may have been truly atrocious and hateful, but in God's estimation, this person's soul is still infinitely precious and worth pursuing for the kingdom.

Yourself. You are redefined, no longer the victim of a senseless act of wickedness but a child who is under the care and guidance of a loving Father with very high standards. Your trials refine you with challenges to resist sin so that you may be holy, just as your Father is holy.[7] Whether God sends trials your way or merely allows you to experience the consequences of living in a world corrupted by sin, He is nevertheless with you in the fire that tempers you; He holds you fast when floods of despair threaten to overwhelm you; He protects you by limiting your testing to only what you can endure.[8] Furthermore, the wounding event places you in a unique position to minister to others, even — *especially* — the person who wounded you. As God loves and comforts you, you in turn can offer His love and comfort to others who are troubled.[9] The good gifts you receive from heaven are always meant to be shared.

Finally, when you release your offender from blame, you free yourself to "run the race" God has set before you. In fixing your eyes on Jesus, instead of on your offender, you can at last move on from your injury into a future where God has specifically called you…

…to belong to Christ.
…to be a saint.
…to live according to His purpose.
…to be a child of the living God.

...to be holy.

...to have fellowship with Jesus.

...to live in peace.

...to look to others' interests as well as your own.

...to bless others as you have been blessed.

...to be loved by God.

...to be free.

...to know hope.

...to share in the glory of Jesus Christ.

...to be of a royal priesthood and a holy nation.

...to live in God's wonderful light.

...to follow in Christ's footsteps.

...to be Christ's chosen and faithful follower.

...to be obedient.

...to complete the task God has assigned to you.[10]

Today's Fitness Challenge - Day 5

☑ FEED YOUR SOUL: *"And we know that in all things God works for the good of those who love him, who have been called according to his purpose."*

—Romans 8:28

☑ LISTEN TO FORGIVENESS: Releasing my offender from blame releases me to do the work God has planned for me.

☑ CHECK YOUR HEART: When has God worked for my good through a painful situation?

☑ KEEP GOING: With God's help, I will focus less on my offender's guilt and more on Jesus and following in His footsteps.

Bonus Challenge

1. How is holding others accountable for their actions different from blaming them for my suffering? Does blaming others relieve my suffering? What helped Jesus to endure His suffering on the cross?

2. What memories or feelings have I tried to avoid by staying angry? What would happen if I acknowledged these memories or feelings?

3. Have I ever blamed others unfairly? What prompted me to make these false accusations? Is there anyone to whom I should apologize?

Week Five
My Fitness Log

☑ *Complete each statement as found in the lesson indicated.* *

1. Forgiveness becomes a _____ as you apply _____ _____ to your daily habits. *(DAY 1)*

2. A _____ _____ grows stronger with _____. *(DAY 1)*

3. _____ families _____ their members, some more than others and in different ways. *(DAY 2)*

4. Most _____ with people in general, not just with family members, begin with _____ _____. *(DAY 2)*

5. Quarrels and conflicts can be useful because they _____ our _____ _____. *(DAY 3)*

6. ____ _____ is always my choice. *(DAY 3)*

7. Forgiveness is _____ a free pass to _____ offensive or destructive behaviors. *(DAY 4)*

8. Forgiving brings _____ _____ into dark places. *(DAY 4)*

9. Perhaps surprisingly, _____ _____ is an important and necessary step in the process of forgiving. *(DAY 5)*

10. _____ blaming undermines our ability to _____ from an injury. *(DAY 5)*

* See Appendix A for answer key.

☑ Record the most important lesson you learned this week.

☑ Write a prayer to God. Tell Him truthfully what is in your heart at this stage of your walk and ask Him for what you need to continue.

Week Five
Weekend Workout

Forgiveness Action Plan

THE WARM-UP. Read aloud from Psalm 25:

> OF DAVID.
>
> *To you, O LORD, I lift up my soul;*
> *in you I trust, O my God.*
> *Do not let me be put to shame,*
> *nor let my enemies triumph over me.*
> *No one whose hope is in you*
> *will ever be put to shame,*
> *but they will be put to shame*
> *who are treacherous without excuse.*
>
> *Show me your ways, O LORD,*
> *teach me your paths;*
> *guide me in your truth and teach me,*
> *for you are God my Savior,*
> *and my hope is in you all day long.*
>
> *— Psalm 25:1-5*

THE STRETCH. Read the psalm again but this time silently and prayerfully. Ask the Holy Spirit to pray through the psalm with you.

How is God's view of shame different from what the world views as shameful?

How does God guide you in His truth and teach you the

paths He wants you to follow?

THE WORKOUT. The path to Christian maturity is as individual as your thumbprint. God created each person to be different, and your life experiences are unlike anyone else's. He designed your particular temperament and personality and then placed you in an environment where people and events molded your childhood experience in such a way that you arrived at adulthood already on a path that you alone could travel. You may have known God as a child, or perhaps you met Him later. Your childhood may have been safe, protected by loving adults, or you may have been abused and neglected and learned early how to survive in a hostile world. Every experience in your life has brought you to where you are today; helpful or hurtful, each event has contributed to shaping the way you cope with conflict and your willingness to forgive those who mistreat you.

Although your path to spiritual maturity is unique, you nevertheless share kingdom principles with all believers. Spiritual practices, set out in Scripture, help to keep you on the path and moving in the right direction:

Obeying God's laws.
Listening for the Spirit.
Reading God's Word.
Examining your heart.
Confessing and repenting your sins.
Training your eyes on Christ's example.
Hoping in the promise of eternal life.
Being assured of your inheritance.
Living as a citizen of God's kingdom in this world.
Humbling yourself.
Giving thanks every day.

As part of your spiritual journey, learning to forgive also depends upon kingdom principles and practices to help keep you on the right track. Below is a worksheet to help you work through any wounding event in a way that honors God and brings you closer to forgiveness. The process follows three steps: exploring the event from different perspectives, considering new insights, and seeking God's counsel in deciding upon a new course of action.

Forgiveness Action Plan

Choose a specific wounding event and fill in the worksheet below. Try to be objective and thorough as you answer every review question that applies. (You may not know the answers to some questions.) Blank spaces have been left for you to add questions of your own. Follow up with Step 2 and Step 3 to determine your path to forgiveness.

Today's Date:_____

<u>Step 1</u>: REVIEW

About My Injury:

1. What was the injury?

2. When did it happen?

3. Where did it happen?

4. Who else saw what happened?

5. Who was primarily responsible for hurting me?

6. Who else contributed to my injury? (e.g., others who could have warned me, protected me, helped me afterward, but didn't)

7. Was it personal or impersonal?

8. Was it accidental or intentional?

9. Was anyone else a victim?

10. Did it happen more than once?

11.

12.

About Myself:
13. How old was I?

14. What did I feel at the time?

15. What do I feel about it now?

16. In what ways did I suffer at the time?

17. How do I still suffer because of the injury?

18. Was I responsible in any way for what happened to me?

19. How accurate is my memory of the injury?

20. How did I react to what happened?

21. Did I tell anyone about it? What did I say?

22. Does my memory agree with what others remember about the incident?

23. How did the injury affect me emotionally?

24. How did the injury affect my ability to trust?

25. How did the injury affect my relationship with my offender?

26. How did the injury affect my other relationships?

27. How did the injury affect my feelings about God?

28. What has the injury cost me financially?

29. Did I feel personally betrayed?

30. What did I lose because of what happened to me?

31. What do I wish I had done that I didn't do?

32. What do I wish others had done that they didn't do?

33. Have I ever been tempted to injure others in the same way that my offender injured me?

34.

35.

About My Offender:
36. What was my offender's full name?

37. How old was my offender?

38. What was my relationship with my offender?

39. How close did I feel to my offender at the time of the injury?

40. Was my offender a follower of Christ?

41. Did my offender have any physical problems?

42. Did my offender have any mental problems?

43. How emotionally isolated was my offender?

44. Did my offender have heavy stressors at the time? (e.g., divorce, illness, job loss, family difficulties, financial hardships)

45. What was my offender's childhood like?

46. Who were my offender's role models?

47. Was my offender's self-concept mostly positive or negative?

48. Did my offender have personal dreams that were never realized?

49. Why do I think my offender acted against me?

50. Did my offender express remorse?

51. Has my offender made efforts to change?

52. What is one quality that I admire about my offender?

53. What do I most dislike about my offender?

54. Did my offender have addictive behaviors?

55. Is there a quality in my offender that I also see in myself?

56. How would God describe my offender?

57. Why would God want to save my offender?

58. What sort of temperament and personality was my offender probably born with?

59.

60.

About My Forgiving:
61. How do I feel about forgiving my offender?

62. How do I feel about God's forgiving my offender?

63. Am I more inclined to obsess about the injury or to push it completely out of my mind?

64. How well can I distinguish between the injury I suffered and the person who caused the injury?

65. What is most unforgivable about my offender?

66. Do I sometimes believe that I could forgive my offender?

67. What would I risk by feeling compassion for my offender?

68. Do I believe that forgiving my offender is the same as excusing the injury?

69. Do I believe that forgiveness means my suffering didn't matter?

70. Do I believe that my withholding forgiveness makes my offender suffer?

71. Have I grieved for what the injury cost me?

72. What would others think of me if I forgave my offender?

73. How would I extend forgiveness to my offender?

74. How would my offender likely respond to my offer of forgiveness?

75. Have I promised anyone, including myself, that I would punish my offender?

76. What are my fantasies for revenge?

77. How attached am I to my role as a victim?

78. Have I become addicted to my pain, anger, or depressed mood?

79. Is there anything about my offender that I could forgive right now?

80. How would my life change if I could let go of this injury?

81. Do I want to be reconciled with my offender?

82. If my offender and I were to reconcile, how would our relationship be different than it was before the injury?

83. If reconciliation were not possible or advisable, would I still be willing to forgive my offender?

84. How would forgiving my offender affect my relationship with God?

85. What would it take before I could trust my offender once again?

86. How does this injury affect other relationships in my life right now?

87. If I could let go of my anger, what emotion would likely take its place?

88.

89.

Step 2: REFLECT
What insights did I gain from answering the review questions?

What I learned about my injury:

What I learned about myself:

What I learned about my offender:

What I learned about my forgiving:

Step 3: RESOLVE

Take some time right now to pray. Offer to God your injury, your new insights, and your heart. Ask Him to teach you the path that He wants you to follow in this matter.

As the Spirit leads you, write down what God is directing you to do.

THE COOL-DOWN. Reflect on your process of working through your Forgiveness Action Plan. Which questions were most difficult to answer? Go back now and mark them; as you use the worksheet to process other injuries, notice which questions consistently challenge you. Next, consider your responses to Step 2 and Step 3. How might you have responded differently at the beginning of your walk with forgiveness?

Your five-week study has taken you through an intense series of topics, perhaps challenging and sometimes painful. Take time now to recognize your accomplishment and appreciate your progress! Don't forget to thank God for His refining work in you. Remember to trust Him always—as the Father who loves you beyond all measure, He will give you the grace and courage you need to continue walking in the Spirit and with forgiveness.

> *Be joyful. Grow to maturity. Encourage each other. Live in harmony and peace.*
> *Then the God of love and peace will be with you.*
> *— 2 Corinthians 13:11 (NLT)*

APPENDIX A

"My Fitness Log" Answer Key

Week One

1. To forgive is to <u>act</u> on the decision to <u>bless</u> and <u>not</u> <u>curse</u> your offender.

2. To the extent that I feel <u>loved</u> and <u>forgiven</u> by God, I can <u>love</u> and <u>forgive</u> others.

3. When God asks you to forgive, He will <u>always</u> give you the <u>grace</u> and the <u>goodness</u> to do it.

4. God blesses me <u>twice</u> when I share <u>His</u> <u>goodness</u> with others.

5. Learning to forgive means learning to rely more and more on <u>God's</u> <u>ways</u> and less on <u>our</u> <u>natural</u> <u>inclinations</u>.

6. I make my own suffering <u>worse</u> when I allow <u>bitter</u> <u>roots</u> to take hold of my heart.

7. For God called you to <u>do</u> <u>good</u>, even if it means <u>suffering</u>, just as Christ suffered for you.

8. When I act on my <u>decision</u> to forgive, Christ's goodness <u>becomes</u> <u>visible</u> in me.

9. Forgiveness is always about <u>people</u>.

10. Old <u>resentments</u> are easily triggered by <u>new</u> <u>events</u>.

Week Two

1. More important than <u>forgiving</u> is learning to <u>love</u> <u>God</u>.

2. <u>Love</u> your enemies and <u>pray</u> for those who persecute you.

3. Every <u>wounding</u> experience places you at a new <u>crossroad</u>.

4. In <u>Christ</u> we have a perfect model of how to <u>respond</u> to <u>wounding</u> events.

5. Draw <u>near</u> to God, and He will <u>draw</u> <u>near</u> to you.

6. Your <u>Enemy</u> is <u>not</u> the person who hurt you.

7. He who <u>conceals</u> his sins does not prosper, but whoever <u>confesses</u> and <u>renounces</u> them finds mercy.

8. Mercy is a <u>gift</u>, not a <u>reward</u>.

9. It is better to suffer for <u>doing good</u>, if suffering should be God's will, than to suffer for <u>doing</u> <u>evil</u>.

10. <u>Withholding</u> forgiveness is a common strategy for responding to relationship pain.

Week Three

1. We must choose between the riches of <u>earthly</u> <u>life</u> or those of <u>God's</u> <u>kingdom</u>.

2. My <u>choices</u> reveal the <u>treasures</u> I have hidden in my heart.

3. Sorrow over our sins can either <u>remake</u> us or <u>destroy</u> us.

4. <u>Hopeless</u> remorse traps me in the past, but <u>hopeful</u> remorse opens me to a different future.

5. As humans, we need to believe <u>that</u> <u>we</u> <u>matter</u>.

6. When people treat us <u>indifferently</u>, they stop <u>reflecting</u> us.

7. God alone is capable of <u>perfect</u> <u>forgiveness</u>.

8. Jesus is both our <u>model</u> and our <u>means</u> for human perfection in the Father.

9. As mercy has been shown to you, go and <u>do</u> <u>likewise</u>.

10. Forgiveness is a <u>job</u> <u>skill</u> that I can <u>learn</u> and <u>practice</u>.

Week Four

1. It's <u>not</u> your job to forgive yourself, but <u>God's</u>.

2. If we truly could <u>forgive</u> our own sins, then we would have <u>no</u> <u>need</u> for a Savior.

3. Inevitably, the <u>sin</u> that cripples us <u>internally</u> will show up in our <u>relationships</u>.

4. The more <u>honest</u> I am with myself, the <u>less</u> <u>fault</u> I find in my neighbor.
5. Decide whether you would rather <u>be</u> <u>right</u> or <u>be</u> <u>reconciled</u>.
6. In a relationship, insisting on being <u>right</u> often means <u>being left</u>.
7. Surrendering your injury to love is <u>deciding</u> to handle your relationship <u>God's</u> <u>way</u>.
8. <u>Surrendering</u> to love gets easier with <u>practice</u>.
9. When you <u>forgive</u> from a changed heart, you offer up a <u>spiritual</u> <u>sacrifice</u> that pleases God.
10. To forgive one another is a <u>priestly</u> privilege and <u>responsibility</u>.

Week Five

1. Forgiveness becomes a <u>lifestyle</u> as you apply <u>kingdom values</u> to your daily habits.
2. A <u>forgiving</u> <u>heart</u> grows stronger with <u>exercise</u>.
3. <u>All</u> families <u>fail</u> their members, some more than others and in different ways.
4. Most <u>quarrels</u> with people in general, not just with family members, begin with <u>unmet</u> <u>expectations</u>.
5. Quarrels and conflicts can be useful because they <u>expose</u> our <u>character</u> <u>flaws</u>.
6. <u>To</u> <u>sin</u> is always my choice.
7. Forgiveness is <u>not</u> a free pass to <u>continue</u> offensive or destructive behaviors.
8. Forgiving brings <u>God's</u> <u>light</u> into dark places.
9. Perhaps surprisingly, <u>affixing</u> <u>blame</u> is an important and necessary step in the process of forgiving.
10. <u>Excessive</u> blaming undermines our ability to <u>recover</u> from an injury.

APPENDIX B

"Weekend Workout" Answers and Supplements

FORGIVENESS APTITUDE (*Weekend Workout* for Week One)
Inventory statements are numbered and grouped by Asset
Category:

CHRISTIAN WORLDVIEW
1 — God is the creator and sovereign Lord of everything in the
world.
21 — Hurting others is wrong because it violates God's laws.
41 — God cares about my enemies as much as He cares about me.
61 — Satan is a real and powerful source of evil in our world.
11 – People deserve the bad things that happen to them.
*31 – The presence of evil in the world is proof that God is not in
control.*
*51 – Once I have been saved by Jesus, I am free to behave any way I
want.*
71 – Truth is relative, defined by time and culture.

COMPASSION
2 — Mercy is more important than justice.
22 — I always knew my family would love me no matter what I
did.
42 — I notice when others are suffering, and I want to help them.
62 — I enjoy serving the needs of others.
12 – I don't forgive, and I don't expect others to forgive me.
32 – I pride myself on being a perfectionist.
52 – Compassion clouds my judgment and keeps me from doing what's

necessary.

72 – People suffer afflictions because God is punishing them.

CONNECTEDNESS

3 – I tend to give people the benefit of the doubt.

23 – I enjoy being with others, and I also enjoy being alone.

43 – I have built-in needs for relationship.

63 – People often ask me for help.

13 – I am not good at making or keeping friends.

33 – If others knew who I really am, they would not like me.

53 – Strong people meet their own needs without relying on others.

73 – People will take advantage of me if they get the chance.

DEVOTION TO GOD

4 – Every day I try to be more like Christ.

24 – I feel God's presence in my life.

44 – I show my love for God by loving other people.

64 – I am God's person.

14 – God loves others more than He loves me.

34 – God is distant, judging, and frankly unlikable.

54 – I cannot forgive God for letting me down.

74 – I cannot love a God who won't protect innocent people from being hurt.

EMOTIONAL DISCIPLINE

5 – I allow myself to feel angry or sad, but the feelings eventually pass.

25 – I am careful in what I say to other people.

45 – I am not one to hold a grudge.

65 – It's okay to be angry at someone I love.

15 – I enjoy the rush I get when I feel angry and powerful.

35 – My being sick or depressed gets me out of my responsibilities.

55 – Crying makes me uncomfortable, whether it's my crying or

someone else's.
75 — I have a hard time identifying my feelings.

HUMILITY

6—I will never be good enough on my own to earn a place in God's kingdom.

26—God is the source of everything good in my life.

46—I readily apologize when I realize that I have been wrong.

66— I am good at seeing things from another person's point of view.

16 — I react defensively when someone criticizes me.

36 — I feel compelled to share my opinion whether or not others ask for it.

56 — I am a master at one-upmanship.

76 — I have been described as boastful.

INTEGRITY

7—Honesty is always the best policy.

27—I am always the same person no matter what situation I am in.

47—I refuse to pass along rumors about people even when I think the rumors are true.

67—I make promises carefully, and I always keep them.

17 — I don't mind intimidating people when I know I'm right.

37 — It's okay to cheat as long as I don't hurt anyone.

57 — It is pointless to feel remorse over something that cannot be changed.

77 — I misrepresent myself to others because I want them to accept me.

RESILIENCE

8—No matter how bad things get, I always have choices.

28—What I have suffered gives me special gifts for helping others.

48 — At least one person loved and believed in me when I was growing up.

68 — I am confident that I will spend eternity with God.

18 – I am easily discouraged.

38 – Life makes no sense to me.

58 – I cannot imagine living a different life.

78 – I don't trust myself to make the right choices.

SELF-ACCEPTANCE

9 — God takes special delight in me.

29 — I am comfortable with making mistakes.

49 — I have no qualms about saying No to people.

69 — I take care of my body by eating well and exercising regularly.

19 – I am too ashamed to admit when I am wrong.

39 – I am damaged goods.

59 – I have thought about harming myself.

79 – I learned to hide my real self from others when I was growing up.

SPIRITUAL PRACTICE

10 — God has answered my prayers.

30 — I feel close to God in nature.

50 — I pray, fast, meditate, or study the Bible to get closer to God.

70 — I confess my sins and ask God to forgive me.

20 – Worshipping God seldom touches me on a personal level.

40 – I have no sense of God working in my life.

60 – Praying to God doesn't work for me.

80 – I have little interest in reading the Bible.

TRUTH OR MYTH? (*Weekend Workout* for Week Three)

Answers and rationale are provided for each quiz statement:

M   1.   My forgiveness is not complete until the other person accepts it.
My forgiveness is entirely within my control, regardless of how the other person responds to me.

T   2.   Forgotten offenses have the power to hurt us in the present.
Unless they have been acknowledged and healed, forgotten offenses can continue to hurt us.

M   3.   Forgiveness is the first step in healing from an intimate wound.
Forgiveness is one of the final steps in healing from an intimate wound.

M   4.   When I forgive, I am saying that the offense no longer matters.
When I forgive, I am saying that although the offense may matter very much, the person who hurt me matters more.

M   5.   Some offenses are so hurtful that nothing good can come from them.
We can choose to learn from our experiences, and the painful lessons often teach us the most.

M   6.   Everyone deserves a chance to be forgiven, no matter what the offense.
No one deserves to be forgiven, and that's the point — forgiveness is a gift of mercy given to one who deserves punishment.

M   7.   Holding onto my anger and bitterness protects me from further hurt.
Clinging to my anger and bitterness makes me suffer in other ways and keeps me from recovering from the injury.

M   8.   The other person should understand my hurt without my having to explain it.

I cannot assume that others understand my feelings unless I explain them.

T   9.   Forgiving does not necessarily mean trusting the other person again.
I can forgive even if I no longer trust the other person.

M   10.   Although I may not get one, I deserve an apology from the person who offended me.
Apologies make forgiveness and reconciliation easier; however, like forgiveness, an apology is a gift.

M   11.   Reconciliation is not possible until both parties acknowledge their own guilt.
I can reconcile with another even if we never agree on who was the more guilty. He may never see himself as guilty, and I may have taken offense because of another wound already in me that was triggered.

M   12.   I cannot approach God in prayer if I am still angry with my offender.
I can approach God in prayer anytime, and especially when I need help forgiving.

M   13.   Forgiving a loved one is easier than forgiving a stranger.
Forgiving a stranger is typically easier than forgiving someone who betrayed my trust and love.

T   14.   Some offenses are unforgivable.
Although an offense may be terrible and unforgivable, no person is unforgivable.

M   15.   If I forgive an unrepentant offender, then I am shirking my moral responsibility to bring him or her to justice.
The notion that I am punishing an offender by withholding forgiveness is an illusion. My first moral responsibility is to acknowledge the reality of the offender's innate worth as a child of God.

M   16.   The bigger the offense, the harder it is to forgive.

Sometimes a small offense may trigger a deep wound already inside me, making it difficult for me to forgive.

M   17.   Forgiving gives permission for the other person to continue the offensive behavior.
Forgiveness discourages offensive behavior by calling attention to it, naming it, and recasting it in a moral context as wrong or hurtful.

M   18.   Until the other person understands my perspective, I cannot fully heal from the offense.
I require nothing from the other person in order to heal from the offense and let go of my resentment.

M   19.   Memories of minor offenses may change over time, but memories of deep wounds remain intact.
All memories change with time and especially those that we revisit often.

T   20.   The goal of forgiveness is always reconciliation.
The goal of forgiveness is always to restore and heal a broken relationship. Restoration is not always possible, but the very nature of forgiveness is always hopeful and reparative.

M   21.   Withholding forgiveness gives me power in the relationship.
My holding onto a grudge gives the other person power over me.

M   22.   In forgiving, I give up the hope that the other person will repent.
Forgiveness may encourage repentance by shining God's light in a dark situation.

M   23.   Forgiving someone conditionally is better than not forgiving at all.
Conditional forgiveness is not really forgiveness but a power game.

M   24. Forgiving makes me vulnerable to the other person.
Forgiveness puts me in charge of my own feelings and responses in a relationship.

M   25. Forgiveness is self-sacrificing.
In forgiving, I refuse to sacrifice any more of myself — my feelings, my power, or my life — to the hurtful experience. Moreover, I open myself to a larger life unrestricted by bitterness and the need for revenge.

M   26. If I wait long enough, a damaged relationship will usually heal itself.
Left unattended, a damaged relationship tends to get worse.

M   27. Forgiving another person tears down the personal boundaries between us.
Forgiving the other person clarifies the personal boundaries between us. I can only forgive when I understand our separateness.

M   28. Only through forgiveness can a damaged relationship return to the way it was before the rift.
A damaged relationship can never go back to exactly the way it was before the rift. Hopefully, a healed relationship will be stronger and more satisfying.

T   29. Wanting to promote my own well-being is a legitimate reason to forgive.
Wanting to heal my own heart is one of the best reasons for deciding to forgive.

M   30. When two people fight, it is usually clear which person is the victim and which is the offender who needs forgiving.
When two people fight, each typically feels in some way victimized by the other.

APPENDIX C

Suggestions for Small Group Study

Your five-week walk with forgiveness adapts well to small group study. Partnering with other Christians will keep you strong and focused as you navigate difficult and sometimes painful topics and challenges. You can help each other along by sharing honestly about your insights and experiences with relationship conflict. In a safe and confidential environment, you can be free to express your fears and doubts and to seek help in exposing those spiritual blind spots and weaknesses that have kept you from forgiving.

Sharing the journey with others is your best chance for success. If you are not currently a member of a small group, consider creating one for this five-week study. A suggested plan is for individuals to work through the week of five lessons and Weekend Workshop on their own, answering the challenge questions and praying through the material with the Holy Spirit's guidance. The small group then meets together to discuss the week's material and encourage one another. Your group facilitator can use the schedule below or adapt the weekly material to fit your established small group format.

WEEK ONE

Engage *(15 minutes)*

Each person shares a brief answer to the following questions:

(1) What has been the worst weather or natural disaster in

my experience?

(2) Was I well-equipped or under-equipped to meet the challenge?

Review *(40 minutes)*

Drawing from this week's text, challenge questions, Scripture references, and Weekend Workout, highlight and discuss material that was meaningful to members. Encourage individuals to share new insights and experiences with forgiveness.

Explore *(20 minutes)*

Read Ephesians 6:10-17.

Discuss the following questions:

(1) How does each element of God's armor help me to forgive?

(2) How have I armored myself with the wrong elements?

(3) How does each wrong element block my ability to forgive?

Pray *(15 minutes)*

Include the following three points in your prayer time together:

(1) Honor God for who He is.

(2) Thank God for providing the armor you need to forgive others.

(3) Ask God to help you discard the armor that keeps you from forgiving.

WEEK TWO

Engage *(15 minutes)*

Each person shares a brief answer to the following questions:

(1) Who cared for my physical needs when I was a child?

(2) What was my caregiver's attitude toward serving my

needs?

Review *(40 minutes)*

Drawing from this week's text, challenge questions, Scripture references, and Weekend Workout, highlight and discuss material that was meaningful to members. Encourage individuals to share new insights and experiences with forgiveness.

Explore *(20 minutes)*

Read John 13:1-17.

Discuss the following questions:

(1) Why did Jesus wash Judas's feet when He knew that this disciple would betray Him?

(2) How would I feel about Jesus' washing my dirty feet?

(3) How are serving and forgiving related concepts?

Pray *(15 minutes)*

Include the following three points in your prayer time together:

(1) Honor God for who He is.

(2) Thank God for His gift of Jesus, the willing servant who bought your salvation.

(3) Ask God for opportunities for you to serve that will bring Him glory.

WEEK THREE

Engage *(15 minutes)*

Each person shares a brief answer to the following questions:

(1) What scared me most when I was a child?

(2) To whom did I go for comfort and safety?

Review *(40 minutes)*

Drawing from this week's text, challenge questions, Scripture references, and Weekend Workout, highlight and discuss material that was meaningful to members. Encourage individuals to share new insights and experiences with forgiveness.

Explore *(20 minutes)*

Read Genesis 3:1-13 and 1 John 4:18.

Discuss the following questions:

(1) Why does my "nakedness" make me afraid?

(2) How does fear keep me from forgiving?

(3) What do I risk by not forgiving?

Pray *(15 minutes)*

Include the following three points in your prayer time together:

(1) Honor God for who He is.

(2) Thank God for the perfect love that takes away fear.

(3) Ask God to replace your fears with the hope and love you need to forgive.

WEEK FOUR

Engage *(15 minutes)*

Each person shares a brief answer to the following questions:

(1) Who was my best friend when I was growing up?

(2) How did we express our solidarity as friends?

Review *(40 minutes)*

Drawing from this week's text, challenge questions, Scripture references, and Weekend Workout, highlight and discuss material that was meaningful to members. Encourage individuals to share new insights and experiences with forgiveness.

Explore *(20 minutes)*

Read John 17:20-26, Psalm 133:1-3, and 1 John 4:7-12.

Discuss the following questions:

(1) Why is unity among believers so important to God?

(2) What is the greatest unifying force among God's people?

(3) Who suffers when believers refuse to forgive one another?

Pray *(15 minutes)*

Include the following three points in your prayer time together:

(1) Honor God for who He is.

(2) Thank God for the gift of Christian community.

(3) Ask God for the loving desire you need to forgive your brothers and sisters in Christ.

WEEK FIVE

Engage *(15 minutes)*

Each person shares a brief answer to the following questions:

(1) What was the one thing I yearned as a child to do when I became a grownup?

(2) How has my perception of that one thing changed since I became an adult?

Review *(40 minutes)*

Drawing from this week's text, challenge questions, Scripture references, and Weekend Workout, highlight and discuss material that was meaningful to members. Encourage individuals to share new insights and experiences with forgiveness.

Explore *(20 minutes)*

Read Philippians 3:12-16 and James 1:2-4.

Discuss the following questions:

(1) Are spiritual maturity and perfection the same thing?

(2) How do relationship conflicts test my faith and develop

perseverance?

(3)   Why is forgiveness essential to spiritual maturity?

Pray *(15 minutes)*

Include the following three points in your prayer time together:

(1)   Honor God for who He is.

(2)   Thank God for His Spirit, who guides you toward spiritual maturity.

(3)   Ask God for the grace and humility to accept His refining influence in your life.

Notes

WEEK ONE
What Is Forgiveness?
1. Colossians 3:13
2. Luke 6:35–36(NRSV)

Bless Your Persecutors
1. 1 Corinthians 10:13; Titus 1:2
2. Romans 5:10
3. Colossians 2:13
4. 1 Corinthians 6:19
5. 1 Peter 2:9
6. Matthew 5:3-10
7. Revelation 7:17
8. 2 Corinthians 1:3–4
9. Matthew 11:29
10. 1 Corinthians 5:5
11. Psalm 51:10
12. Ephesians 2:14-22

Bitter Roots
1. Romans 12:14
2. Romans 7:18
3. Matthew 5:3-10

Do Good
1. Romans 12:14
2. James 2:17-18 (MSG)

3. Luke 22:62
4. Mark 16:7
5. Colossians 3:5-11

Forgiveness Aptitude
1. Mark 11:15-17
2. Hebrews 4:15

WEEK TWO
Begin with God
1. Matthew 23:27–28
2. Deuteronomy 6:4–9
3. Leviticus 19:18
4. 1 John 4:7–21
5. Exodus 20:4
6. Exodus 20:13
7. Exodus 20:16
8. Matthew 5:44

The Cross at the Crossroad
1. Luke 23:34
2. Galatians 5:19–21
3. Galatians 5:22

Meet the Enemy
1. Ephesians 2:2 (TLB)
2. 2 Peter 3:9
3. Galatians 5:17

4. Luke 6:27–31
5. Romans 12:20
6. Proverbs 24:17
7. Romans 5:6 (TLB)

How Much Is Enough?
1. Galatians 5:22

Forgiveness Prayer
1. Luke 11:1
2. Matthew 6:9-13

WEEK THREE
Hidden Treasures
1. Luke 12:34
2. Ephesians 4:32

Hopeful Remorse
1. 2 Chronicles 33:2
2. 2 Chronicles 33:9
3. 2 Chronicles 33:13 (NLT)

Indifference Hurts
1. Matthew 27:46
2. 1 John 1:9

The Perfect Goal
1. James 1:25; 2 Samuel
   22:31; Psalm 18:30;
   Deuteronomy 32:4
2. Hebrews 2:10
3. Philippians 3:20-21
4. 1 John 4:16

5. Psalm 136 (NRSV)
6. Matthew 5:9
7. Hebrews 10:14

Called to God's Business
1. Luke 6:36
2. James 2:5
3. Isaiah 66:2
4. Micah 6:8
5. 2 Thessalonians 1:11

Truth or Myth?
1. Proverbs 9:10 (NLT)
2. 1 Corinthians 13:12;
   Romans 1:24–32
3. 1 Corinthians 1:20

WEEK FOUR
Can I Forgive Myself?
1. Luke 10:27
2. Matthew 6:12
3. John 8:11 (NAS)

A Little Yeast
1. Matthew 23:27
2. Matthew 16:6
3. Matthew 23:13 (NLT)
4. Matthew 13:33 (TLB)
5. Romans 12:9; 2
   Corinthians 6:6; 1 Timothy
   1:5; 2 Timothy 1:5; James
   3:17; 1 Peter 1:22
6. Romans 12:9-13,16

7.   2 Corinthians 6:6–7 (NLT)
8.   1 Timothy 1:5 (NLT)
9.   James 3:17–18

When Ends Justify Means
1.   Genesis 37:1–50:26

The Fragrance of Forgiveness
1.   Ephesians 5:2
2.   1 Peter 2:5
3.   John 4:24 (NAS)
4.   Romans 12:1–2
5.   Matthew 18:35

Song to God
1.   Psalm 139:20
2.   Psalm 10:2-11
3.   Psalm 58:3
4.   Psalm 83:3-4; 94:5
5.   Psalm 94:22-23
6.   Psalm 83:16
7.   Psalm 83:17-18
8.   Psalm 6:3
9.   Psalm 135:13-14;
     Deuteronomy 32:35
10. Psalm 35:12-14
11. Psalm 31:17-18
12. Psalm 58:10-11

WEEK FIVE
Ten Habits of Forgiveness
1.   Colossians 3:13 (NRSV)
2.   Psalm 32:1

3.   Matthew 5:23-24 (NCV)
4.   Matthew 5:43-45 (MSG)
5.   Galatians 5:22-23
6.   Proverbs 12:18
7.   Proverbs 18:19 (NCV)
8.   Colossians 1:19-20 (NLT)
9.   Job 6:24-25
10. 1 Peter 5:5 (NRSV)
11. Philippians 2:7
12. 1 John 4:7-8 (NCV)
13. John 15:5 (NCV)

Family Thorns
1.   Genesis 4:8, 37:28-32; 2
     Samuel 13:14, 15:1-12;
     John 7:1-5
2.   Hebrews 2:11 (TNIV)
3.   John 4:13-14
4.   Revelation 21:23
5.   Philippians 4:19
6.   Romans 13:1-6
7.   1 Timothy 1:5
8.   Isaiah 55:8-9
9.   John 16:33

Facing Our Flaws
1.   James 4:1-3
2.   Romans 8:26
3.   2 Corinthians 12:9
4.   Isaiah 64:6
5.   2 Corinthians 4:17
6.   James 1:3
7.   Psalm 26:2

8. 2 Corinthians 1:4
9. Lamentations 3:40
10. 2 Corinthians 8:2
11. Hebrews 12:7-11
12. Romans 12:2
13. Romans 5:10
14. 1 Corinthians 10:13

Forgiving the Unrepentant

1. Luke 17:3-4
2. Genesis 45:1-15
3. Luke 15:20
4. John 8:3-11
5. Mark 2:1-5
6. Matthew 28:10; John 21:15-19
7. John 6:38
8. Romans 5:10; Ephesians 2:1-9
9. Mark 14:36
10. Philippians 4:7
11. 1 Peter 3:9 (NLT)
12. Romans 12:20
13. Galatians 6:1-5

14. Romans 12:19
15. Romans 2:8
16. Psalm 94:3-5 (NLT)
17. Isaiah 55:8-9

Beyond Blame

1. Ephesians 4:31
2. 1 John 2:11
3. Ephesians 1:11
4. James 1:2-4
5. Romans 3:22-23
6. 2 Peter 3:9
7. 1 Peter 1:14-16
8. 1 Corinthians 10:13
9. 2 Corinthians 1:4
10. Romans 1:6, 7; 8:28; 9:26; 1 Corinthians 1:2, 9; 7:15; Philippians 2:4; Galatians 5:13; Ephesians 1:18; 2 Thessalonians 2:14; Hebrews 9:15; 1 Peter 2:9, 21; 3:9; Jude 1; Revelation 19:11; 1 John 5:3; Acts 20:24

Bible Quotation References

Unless otherwise noted, all Scripture quotations are taken from the Holy Bible, New International Version® NIV®. Copyright © 1973, 1978, 1984 by International Bible Society. Used by permission of Zondervan Publishing House. All rights reserved.

Other translations of The Holy Bible have been quoted:

Scripture quotations marked (ESV) are from The Holy Bible, English Standard Version® (ESV®), copyright © 2001 by Crossway Bibles, a publishing ministry of Good News Publishers. Used by permission. All rights reserved.

Scripture quotations marked (KJV) are from The Holy Bible, King James' Version®, copyright © 1947, 1949. Used by permission of A. J. Holman Company.

Scripture quotations marked (MSG) are taken from THE MESSAGE. Copyright © 1993, 1994, 1995, 1996, 2000, 2001, 2002. Used by permission of NavPress Publishing Group.

Scripture quotations marked (NAS) are taken from the New American Standard Bible®, copyright © 1960, 1962, 1963, 1968, 1971, 1972, 1973. Used by permission of The Lockman Foundation. All rights reserved.

Scripture quotations marked (NCV) are from The Holy Bible, New Century Version®, copyright © 1987, 1988, 1991 by Word Publishing, a division of Thomas Nelson, Inc. Used by permission.

Scripture quotations marked (NLT) are taken from The Holy Bible, New Living Translation, copyright © 1996, 2004, 2007 by Tyndale House Foundation. Used by permission of Tyndale

About the Author

Judith Ingram, M.A. earned her counseling degree at Saint Mary's College of California. She is an ordained elder in the Evangelical Presbyterian Church and a graduate of Cornerstone Bible Academy of Livermore, California.

A survivor of childhood abuse herself, she has received awards for her thesis model employing forgiveness in the clinical treatment of adults recovering from abuse. She has presented forgiveness topics at various workshops for counseling centers, counseling classes, professional conferences, women's Christian conferences, and church ministry groups.

She and her husband are lifetime residents of the San Francisco Bay Area. Please visit her at www.judithingram.com.

Acknowledgements

From the beginning this book has been God's project. I am delighted that He invited me to join Him on the journey, and I'm thankful for the many people He sent to help me along the way: Paula Montibeller Bennett, who first introduced me to Jesus when we were in college; Ruth Ann Thompson for her faithful encouragement and unflagging belief in the goodness of forgiveness; Dr. Robert C. Richard, wise counselor who helped me move through the pain of my wounded childhood to find peace and healing; the community of believers at San Ramon Presbyterian Church and Community Presbyterian Church, Danville, many of whom gathered in small groups to walk through drafts of my book and share their insights with me; Erica Hurtado for author photos; Matt Dodge for Website design; Suzanne Woods Fisher, who generously introduced me to her publisher; and the good people at Vinspire Publishing and especially editor-in-chief Dawn Carrington for her gracious mentoring and valuable feedback. Most of all, to my husband Frank, my daughter Melanie, and my son-in-law Erik—you make my life sweet and the journey worthwhile.

Invest in Your Spiritual Life

Draw closer to God

As your heart seeks God, let our devotionals help you on your journey to a closer walk with Him.

For a complete listing of books available, visit our website at www.vinspirepublishing.com.

Find us on Facebook at
www.facebook.com/VinspirePublishing

Follow us on Twitter at
www.twitter.com/vinspire2004

CPSIA information can be obtained at www.ICGtesting.com
Printed in the USA
BVOW01s1426020614

354976BV00002B/6/P